Graham in the 49B Formula 1 Lotus which was to be one of the most successful designs of all time.

MR MONACO
GRAHAM HILL REMEMBERED

TONY RUDLIN
FOREWORD BY H.S.H. PRINCE RAINIER

 Patrick Stephens, Cambridge

First published September 1983
Reprinted November 1983

British Library Cataloguing in Publication Data

Rudlin, Tony
  Mr Monaco.
  1. Hill, Graham, 1929-   2. Automobile racing
  —Biography
  I. Title
  796.7'2'0924   GV1032 H48

  ISBN 0-85059-357-3

Photoset in 11 on 12 Plantin by MJL Typesetting, Hitchin, Herts. Printed in Great Britain on 115 gsm Fineblade coated cartridge by St Edmundsbury Press, Bury St Edmunds, Suffolk, and bound by Hunter & Foulis Ltd, Edinburgh, for the publishers, Patrick Stephens Limited, Bar Hill, Cambridge, CB3 8EL, England.

Contents

*A nice family Graham kept meeting in Monaco.
Princess Caroline, Prince Rainier, the late
Princess Grace, Prince Albert and Princess
Stephanie.*

On the 29th of November 1975 I felt I had lost a friend!

Graham Hill won the Monaco Grand Prix five times: a record still never surpassed. And he had become as attached to Monaco and its Grand Prix, as we, in Monaco, had become attached to him ... nicknamed Mr. Monaco.

I found it always rewarding to meet Graham Hill and talk with him; his interests and his knowledge spread over a vast field of activities. In fact, he was interested in everything that happened, yet concentrating always on his job, so as to do it the best.

I admired his calm views on people and events, his great sense of humour, simplicity, excluding any pomposity or self-satisfaction. It seemed he really thoroughly enjoyed life and what he was doing.

Graham Hill was an extraordinary well balanced person with charm, humour and a generous approach to life and people. A courageous man with a very attractive personality.

All this, and much more, make me deeply regret to be deprived of the pleasure of his company.

RAINIER, Prince de Monaco

Prologue

Trying to write about someone you have known, worked and played with over a number of years is not easy, especially a man like Graham Hill who has accumulated a vast horde of friends, acquaintances and admirers along the way. At first it seems simple, start with what you know and add to it from the knowledge of others . Unfortunately it doesn't work out that way, not if you want to keep away from the clichés and the record books. The friends stay terribly loyal and the record books reflect nothing more than results and tell nothing about the man. What does soon become glaringly obvious is that your subject has a different personality for each acquaintance you question.

It didn't take long to come to the conclusion that the net result of a book composed by a committee of opinions would result in the ill-famed camel rather than a horse of even the most doubtful breeding. The only way was to go it alone and write about the Graham Hill I knew from first hand experience. It was hard to ignore the titbits of non-corroborated tales that came my way or to stop them from influencing what I wanted to say. The result is a very personalised appreciation of the few years that I knew him and the way he appeared to me—hopefully uninfluenced by outside opinions. Certainly it's not, by any means, a complete portrait of this complicated character—but it is a personal one.

Acknowledgements

Autorace: 36 *bottom*; **Daily Express:** 116; **Daily Mail:** 45; **Jutta Fausel:** 41, 138 *top right*; **Max Le Grand:** back cover; **Team Lotus:** front end paper; **Jackie van Nimwagen:** 50; **RAC:** 13 *bottom left*; **HSH Prince Rainier of Monaco:** 4; **Shell photographic service:** 17, 18, 31 *top*; **David Phipps:** front cover, 121, 123; **Nigel Snowdon:** 46, 52, 57, 58 *top*, 64, 127, 130; **Temple Press Ltd:** 29. Special thanks to **Bette Hill** for all her invaluable help.

Whilst every effort has been made to trace the copyright holders for the photographs used in this book in some cases this has proved impossible.

Introduction

Graham Hill was born in a Hampstead nursing home on February 15 1929. He was one of two brothers whose father worked in the Stock Exchange. Graham attended Hendon Secondary School and then studied engineering at Hendon Technical Institute until he was sixteen. He left to become an apprentice with Smiths Industries Ltd. It was during this period, in a motor bike accident, that he put the bend in his left leg which was to give him the appearance of being bandy. Qualified, he was pounced on by His Majesty's Government to undertake his two years' National Service, which had been deferred while he finished his training. Graham chose the Royal Navy and was accepted as an Engine Room Artificer. Confirmed in the rank of Petty Officer he joined HMS *Swiftsure*. On a courtesy visit to the Mediterranean in 1951, he had his first taste of Monte Carlo, a town he was to become the master of in years to come.

In spite of his interest in things mechanical, Graham didn't get around to driving a car until he was twenty-four, in 1953, and then it was in a beaten up Morris 8 nearly as old as he. A few months later, after reading an advertisement, he went to Brands Hatch and sat in a racing car for the first time. April 1954 saw him on the starting grid for the first time in his Formula 3 debut. He finished second in the heat and fourth in the final. Shortly after this he had a meeting with the late Colin Chapman which was to alter his life. Now a tyro racing driver and instructor he felt he should stabilise his domestic life. On August 13 1955 he married Bette Shubrook and took a flat in Belsize Park.

The following year put him on the motor racing map when he narrowly failed to win the Autosport Series Championship in a Lotus. At that time he was working for Lotus primarily as a mechanic, with the promise of a drive when it was practicable. Graham wanted to change that and worked on Colin Chapman until, in 1957, he was signed up as a driver on a regular basis.

His first Grand Prix was at Monaco in 1958 and he finished the season with two championship points. 1959 was a terrible year and the disillusioned Hill left Lotus to join BRM in 1960. The BRMs were not renowned for their fleetness, but had a good rate of reliability. Graham worked hard on getting the car right and in 1962, at Goodwood, he won his first Formula 1 race. The race was marred by the accident that was to put Stirling Moss out of Formula 1 racing. Graham went on to win his first Grand Prix in Holland and finish the season as Champion ahead of Jimmy Clark in a Lotus.

After Jimmy Clark had opened up the Indianapolis 500 in 1965, Graham was determined to do the same. The next year he stood on the winners' rostrum—but not without a good deal of controversy. (It was with the prize money from this race that he bought his Piper Aztec twin-engined aeroplane.) It was also the year that he appeared in John Frankenheimer's epic film about motor racing: *Grand Prix*.

However, Lotus was his first love and since he was not getting much joy at BRM, where he was partnered by pushy young Jackie Stewart, he returned to the Chapman fold as joint Number One with Jimmy Clark in 1967. The Lotus had just started to show the advantage of the new Cosworth engines when, early in 1968, Clark was killed in a Formula 2 race at Hockenheim in West Germany. Graham kept the Lotus pennant flying and captured his second world championship.

His championship year, 1969, was not the high it should have been and finished with his horrendous accident at Watkins Glen in the US Grand Prix. His legs were so badly smashed that his doctors said he would never walk again. But Graham wouldn't listen, and in March 1970, in a Lotus entered by Rob Walker, he lined up for the South African Grand Prix at Kyalami. He finished in

Below *Aged two, Graham gets to grips with the rudiments of pedal power.*

Right *A report to warm any future World Champion's heart.*

MIDDLESEX ~~COUNTY COUNCIL~~
EDUCATION COMMITTEE

HENDON TECHNICAL INSTITUTE
JUNIOR TECHNICAL SCHOOL

STUDENT'S REPORT

Name _Norman_ _Hill_

Half Yr. ending 23rd. Mar. Term 19 45   Absences _5_

Age _16_ Yrs. _1_ Mths.   Form _3.4/t_   Year _3rd_

Height _5_ ft. _10_ ins.   No. in Form _24_   No. in Year _24_

Weight _9_ st. _9_ lbs.   Position in Form _18_   Position in Year _18_

Subject.	Percentage of Marks.	Grade.
English		C
Geography		C
History		
Mathematics		C
Physics		C
Chemistry		D
Mechanics		C
Technical Drawing		B
Engineering Workshop Practice		C +
Woodwork and Pattern Making		B
Physical Training		B

GRADES:

A. Excellent.   C. Moderate.
B. Good.   D. Unsatisfactory.

Remarks: His interest is chiefly in the practical aspect of the school work. Is not lacking in intelligence by any means. Is slipshod but likeable

J. Middleton ____ Form Master.

C. Bucher ____ Head Master.

____ Parent or Guardian.

Next Term Begins _9th Apr 1945_

Above left *Hill in his HMS* Swiftsure *days*

Above *Graham Hill and Bette Shubrook become Mr and Mrs at St James' Church Paddington at 3.15 pm on August 13 1955.*

Left *'Ah, so that's what it's all about!'*

Above right *On holiday on the Welsh Riviera, Rhyl, with the Chapmans in 1955.*

an incredible sixth place. Graham was all the time becoming more of a public figure and in 1971 was given the Guild of Professional Toast Masters award for the best after dinner speaker.

Courageously ignoring pain, he entered the 1972 Le Mans race in a Matra with co-driver Henri Pescarola. They won, and Graham became the only holder of motor racing's triple crown; the Grand Prix Championship, Indy 500 and Le Mans 24 hour race.

Not satisfied with his racing performance, Graham decided to set up his own team and in 1973 with the sponsorship of WD and HO Wills, he set up the Embassy team. Success eluded him and in 1975, at Silverstone, he retired to concentrate on being team manager to his fast-improving team. He was never to get the success his hard work promised.

Returning from a test session at the Paul Ricard circuit in Southern France in the Piper Aztec, the aircraft plunged into a golf course at Arkley, three miles short of Elstree Airfield.

All five members of his team, Tony Brise, Andy Smallman, Terry Richards, Ray Brimble and Tony Alcock, were killed. It was November 29 1975.

Chapter 1

Over the top

'Greatness' is a matter of time and place, the label is bestowed after a comparison of contemporaries, which uses as a touchstone the effect a man has on his surroundings. Without the evil genius of Hitler, Churchill would probably have drifted off into the failed politicians' limbo, remembered only for such anecdotal events as the Sydney Street siege and his escape from the Boer concentration camp. If Elvis Presley hadn't been able to attract such a sycophantic following for rock and roll, he would probably be an ageing club owner now, doing his thing for bored Saturday night audiences whether they liked it or not.

In the field of motor racing, endless arguments are put forward to assign the crown to various claimants, from Caracciola through Fangio to Emerson Fittipaldi. A good defence can be mounted for any of the claims, but, taking the three quoted, there remains one insurmountable flaw when advancing any argument based on drivers' merits; they never raced against each other and even if they had been pole position rivals there would remain the big enigma of the car, though a really top class driver seems to be able to work miracles with whatever car he happens to drive. In fact, it often seems that drivers become champions in spite of their vehicles. If you put Fangio in the latest Williams or Brabham, he would probably be showing his compatriot Reutemann the way home. But this is unprovable. A yardstick must therefore be applied so that Fangio's chances in a modern Formula 1 car can be judged against those of contemporaries such as Hill, Stewart, Clark, Brabham, Surtees, Rindt and Fittipaldi.

How does twice World Champion Graham Hill stand in the company of his peers? Some time has elapsed since that fatal day in November 1975 when a miscalculation or mischance ploughed Hill and his Embassy team into a tree, on the end of Arkley golf course, killing them all outright. That time has given us the necessary perspective to see clearly the vital role which Hill played in the new era of motor racing which was ushered in at the beginning of 1968 when the CSI (*Commission Sportif International*) gave its blessing, from its prestigious offices in the Place de la Concorde, to commercial sponsorship. Overnight the scene was transformed. Turned back caps were straightened or exchanged for City bowlers. Mechanics' grubby, oil-stained overalls gleamed and the glamorous groupies who circulated amongst the wealthy, playboy drivers became wives or got seconded on to the expense account sheet of the sponsoring firm as 'hostesses'.

Surveying the scene, the image builders didn't find a lot to give them joy.

Jackie Stewart, the glib Scot with lightning reflexes, tried to measure up but out of his car he wasn't impressive. Everybody liked Jimmy Clark, quiet and friendly he was everybody's idea of the boy next door, only nobody seemed to live next door to him. He was a racers'-racer who never sought the adulation of the public who waited to adore him. Three times World Champion Jack Brabham might have served as a symbol of the corporate image. His beetle-browed solemnity seemed well-suited to a pin-striped suit and a darkening oil painting in the board-room. But that wasn't the image which was needed! Taciturn Jochen Rindt wasn't even in the game. Rather than go out shaking hands and smiling he preferred games of rummy. This was a pity because he had the essential accompaniment to a popular star—a beautiful photogenic wife. Unfortunately he wasn't to survive long enough to get into the real money, which made world champions automatic multi-millionaires overnight. Emerson Fittipaldi cornered the market in his own part of the world and dazzled the race fans for four meteoric years before running out of fizz and trailing his spent rocket around the circuits.

The year of transition, 1968, held out false promises and only brought confusion. Exactly what sort of advertising was going to be allowed on the cars was a tricky problem which neither the CSI nor its parent, the FIA, were prepared to take on. No clear mandate had been laid down. Sponsors looked at

Below left *Graham explains the principle of getting past a slower car by going over the top. HRH Prince Charles, Lord Mountbatten and the Duke of Kent look doubtful at the British Grand Prix in 1968.*
Below right *Jo Bonnier, Graham Hill and Dan Gurney eyeing each other uneasily.*

what was going on in other sports and decided to do the same—but more so! New colour schemes replaced the drab national uni-colours promulgated in CSI regulations and brought a new excitement to the tracks. First off the mark was Graham Hill's own Alma Mater, Lotus. Instead of the dull olive green livery relieved by a yellow stripe, which the British team had been saddled with for so long, they roared on to the tarmac in the becoming red, white and gold of their new sponsor, Gold Leaf.

It wasn't to be that easy. Television, little as it covered motor racing, was shocked. They couldn't allow their lenses to be sullied by advertising. It became so difficult at times that the Gold Leaf men had to cover up their well-known symbol or risk the TV reporters flouncing off in shocked outrage. It seemed that the options were advertising revenue or TV coverage. A cruel choice, as the elimination of the latter meant the loss of the former. Escalating costs had pushed the cost of putting a competitive car on the track beyond the budget of trade sponsors, and the transfusion from less committed, more commercial houses was the only way to survive, but they were investing for their commercial health, not to provide toys for playboys. They wanted the spin-off media coverage, and by 'media' they meant television. Without it they would direct their affluence elsewhere.

A secondary problem was convincing would-be backers that they had anything to gain from printing their product's name, in regulation 4 ins letters, on the side of a low-slung glass-fibre tube circulating at 150 mph in front of crowds which rarely exceeded 50,000 and which were more interested in what relish they should put on their hamburger than in the cars themselves. Although budgets were minuscule in comparison with today's, each possibility was tracked to its lair and an amateurish attempt was made to lure the reluctant sponsor into the killing ground. The sponsor was considered a necessary evil who must be stripped of his assets and then made to stand in the corner of the pit while the real 'pros' spent the money. The teams felt that they were doing the commercial people a favour in letting them get within scheckle-throwing distance of their cars.

By the start of the season, in 1969, the middlemen were stirring. Big money is its own fertiliser and from it sprang forth the Mr Fix-its ready to match boardroom with workshop, for a very moderate fee of course. From all the confusion and instant hatred that rumbled over the darkened scene at that time, a pattern started to emerge. If you wanted to run a successful team you had to have a pipeline into the tobacco companies. Players, Marlboro and Kent were the pathfinders and gave sponsorship the million dollar burnish that enticed in the more wary. Yardley, a subsidiary of British American Tobacco, arrived in a blaze of publicity that set the standard for team launches and buried forever the motor racing belief that a dingy, corrugated iron garage and jugs of bitter were suitable accompaniments to the birth of a new challenger for excellence.

The media tried hard, in those two traumatic introductory years, to introduce a new personality to the public. Although Graham Hill had long been the leading light in the rugged social scene, he had one slight flaw as far as the image

Relaxing in Majorca in September 1964.

conscious PR men were concerned. He was old (forty) . . . and he didn't smoke! On the positive side he did have a lot going for him. He looked right. He was the quintessential Englishman as perceived by foreigners and conceived in the *Daily Mirror* cartoon 'Just Jake', with the upper class cad, Captain Reilly Ffowl. Reilly Ffowl could have been the template from which Hill was cut. Both had an irascible nature which grated on those around them but was redeemed by a spirit and sense of occasion which provoked a charge in their vicinity that energised those who came within range. However, Graham lacked the upper class background that Reilly Ffowl claimed.

Graham Hill's rise to international stardom via the Royal Navy, the London Rowing Club and a pound's worth of driving lessons at Brands Hatch at the same age as Fitipaldi won his first Grand Prix two decades later, is well known.

Proof of his stubborness and bloody-minded insistence on getting what he wanted is shown in the way he got a grip on the late Colin Chapman and the infant Lotus in the '50s and bent both to his will. However, Graham's real era in the sun was the early and mid-'60s. With BRM he notched up his first world championship in 1962 and then revived his drooping reputation with a win in the the famous 'Demolition Indy' of 1966. Graham's Indianapolis win was at the end of one of the most spectacular and controversial races ever run. The previous year Colin Chapman, team manager for Lotus, had mounted a calculated onslaught on the 'Brickyard Derby'. The scorn that was poured on his kiddie-car racer by competitors and Press alike almost eclipsed the trauma caused by a crack which appeared in the track surface. Jimmy Clark, driving for Lotus, had good-naturedly let himself be called a rookie and gone along with the jokes. Come the race and he had the ultimate satisfaction of driving the big, specialised American cars into the ground. That was in 1965.

In the year that followed, the Americans took a hard look at their designs and came up with a variety of formulae to make sure that the 'Limeys' didn't steal the headlines again. But now that the dynamic duo of Chapman and Clark had shown what could be done, other UK teams were looking at the racing cornucopia. A win at Indianapolis was as good as a year on the Grands Prix circuit and the natural disdain of the road-runners for the less adventurous circuit races like Indy, with their carefully tailored left hand corners and flat out driving technique, was easily overcome by the sound of distant cash-registers. Lola made Graham an offer he couldn't refuse and, together with Clark and Stewart he turned up for qualification for the 1966 Indy. No exception was made for the World Champion and he ran with the 'rookies'.

No-one was laughing at the little British cars this time. They were the centre of attention but the money went on the Americans in the hope they would pull something out of the bag and restore national pride. There was an uneasy air about the days leading up to the race. Hill reckoned a lot of it was caused by the paddock toilets. Not since his between-deck days in the Navy had he had to suffer the indignity of using 'heads' without doors. And he wasn't averse to saying so whenever he got the opportunity. The privilege of a quiet meditation was restored when, overnight, the race organisers brought the carpenters in and fitted doors. If that had been his only achievement Hill would have felt that he had gained a minor victory. But more was to come. Typically it was not to be easy or without headline controversy.

As the pace-car raced up the slip-road to give the signal for the race to start, 16 cars were wiped out in one metal-bending, wheel-shedding accident, the like of which had never been seen before. In spite of the mechanical carnage there was no significant damage to any of the contestants and, as soon as the remains of many punters' dreams had been swept up, the race was restarted. Graham survived a tricky moment on the first corner when he hit a patch of oil but soon settled down and started moving up through the field. He could hardly believe his luck when he found himself running second to Jackie Stewart after the previous year's winner, Jimmy Clark, had spun out. Then Stewart's engine died and Graham Hill was in the lead, at least that was what his pit board was telling him and he was in no position and had no inclination to argue.

Graham took the chequered flag with his usual aplomb and motored gently around the track accepting the applause, on his way to the winners' enclosure. Unfortunately, Chapman also had Clark cleared for the winners' circle. The crowds were confused when Clark did a lap of honour, waving with all the assurance of a conquering hero retaking the colonies. Graham didn't waste time. As the world Press surged around him, he kissed his way up the huge chequered carpet to receive his just deserts, which, in addition to the not inconsiderable cheque for $160,000, included a glass of milk provided by one of the race sponsors. Jimmy, confused by Chapman's assurance that he was the winner, made his way to the podium. Graham was enjoying himself and nothing was going to cloud his day. When it was suggested that there had been a mix-up in the time-keeper's box Graham brushed it aside and held up the empty milk glass: 'No way!' he cried, 'I've drunk the milk!' A closer scrutiny of Chapman's lap record, compared with the officially composed version, confirmed that Graham's claim would have been valid even if he hadn't drunk the milk!

Challenged by Stewart at BRM and eclipsed by Jimmy Clark driving the more competitive Lotus Climax, Hill moved back to Lotus for the '67 season. Jimmy was well used to his car and team and still managed to show Graham the way round on most occasions. But the ex-rower didn't lack stamina and he stuck there, tailing the more naturally gifted driver and waiting for his opportunity. However, that historic confrontation between Hill the mechanic and Clark the artist, on equal terms, was never to be. It should have happened in 1968.

Mike Costin and Keith Duckworth had put their talents together and created the mighty Ford Cosworth V8 engine, which still dominates international Grands Prix, and Lotus had been let in on the ground floor. Graham had managed to settle back into his old nest at the Lotus factory, now moved to grander quarters at Hethel in Norfolk. Before horns could be locked, Clark was dead, tragically killed by what has often been described as a 'freak' accident in a Formula 2 race at Hockenheim in Germany. (It is a mystery why the accident still seems to puzzle the experts. The car was involved in an accident the week before in Barcelona, and, because of the tightness of the race schedule, there had been no time to test the straightened suspension and chassis properly.) Whatever the reason, Clark was gone and the field was left wide open to Graham Hill.

By the end of 1968 Graham had amassed enough points to take the world championship crown for the second time. He accepted the kudos and the money

The BRM H16 promised a lot but proved too complicated to maintain. In the French Grand Prix of 1966, held at Rheims, Graham never got into the act and retired on lap 12.

but was secretly dissatisfied. His friend and arch rival Clark was dead and Stewart hadn't been competitive for most of the year after a practice shunt in Spain at the beginning of the year had left him nursing a fractured arm. But the media men hadn't Graham Hill's fine sense of values. Hill was Champ! They forgot his age, or perhaps it would be more correct to say that they made his maturity more glamorous. Graham let his thick dark locks grow stylishly long, although he couldn't quite bring himself to indulge in the careless hirsute style that Stewart adopted, and went through a range of colourful shirts which led sceptical eyes away from the grizzled sideburns and the deepening wrinkles.

Ironically, what really put Graham on top of the tinselled PR tree was his horrendous accident at Watkins Glen in the last race of the 1969 Grands Prix season.

Champion though he was, the year had been a poor reflection of his exalted status. He got top marks for endeavour but wise heads around the paddock and in the Press tent nodded sagely and agreed that he was past it. The previous year he had been lucky but now was the time to quit. If he had been younger, the more charitably inclined might have looked for other causes to account for his miserable year; like the punishing round of speeches and parties for the boys he attended, or the fact that Lotus, and Colin Chapman in particular, were still stunned by the death of both Clark and (in practice for the Indy 500) Mike Spence, in the previous year. Chapman's disenchantment meant that the team lost energy and the essential edge in design that they had had when they started Hill's championship chase.

Age was forgotten in the newsworthy copy that Hill's badly shattered legs gave to the Press in the motor racing off season.

A slight mistake had put Hill's Lotus off the road and he had to get out to push it back on the track, a procedure that Graham was famous for and which had preceeded one of his most remarkable victories at Monaco a few years previously. With the new, tailor-made cockpits, it was impossible for the driver to fasten his own seat belt, so he set off in pursuit of the rest of the competitors with the fasteners dangling down beside his legs and draped over his shoulders. He didn't intend to waste time going into the pits to have them fastened if there was a chance that he might salvage something from his disappointing year. Even the fastest lap would be something! A lap later, even that dream began to fade. The handling was going haywire and he soon realised that he had picked up a puncture. It looked as if he would get his safety harness done-up after all. He signalled a flat tyre to his pit crew as he went past so that they would be ready at the end of the next lap. He was nearly round when the unsecured tyre shredded off the hub, dropping the low-slung suspension onto the track. The hard steel

Right *Hill again failed to win the 1966 Grand Prix at Brands Hatch in the heavy weight BRM V8. Minor satisfaction came from beating Clark in the Lotus. Here he rounds Bottom Bend on his way to 3rd place.* **Inset** *Lotus dominated the British Grand Prix at Brands Hatch in July 1968. New boy Jack Oliver (no 9) took over from Hill (no 8) when his drive shaft broke. Jo Siffert came out the winner in the Rob Walker Lotus.*

dug in and negligently flipped the 600 kg Lotus into the air like a discarded plastic toy. Only a few short years earlier the driver's prayer, in this situation, was that he would be thrown well clear of the danger zone. Modern construction made this unlikely. Threaded down under the steering wheel, bracketed and confined by the bulging fuel tanks and shoulder-width sides, there was no natural body movement which would complement the centripetal force and unthread the body. The force was undeniable, it smashed the driver's legs and made it possible for his body to be jettisoned.

Graham's fight back after this disaster was undeniably a stirring example of grit and determination, and was portrayed as such. Hill, sometimes a realist, admitted that without the public's interest he doubted that he would have been able to find the stamina to push himself constantly beyond the pain threshold to be ready for the first Grand Prix of the 1970 season at Kyalami in South Africa. There is no doubt that the epic struggle to prove that he was larger than life, played out in the glare of publicity, gave encouragement and hope to thousands of disabled people who might have been tempted to give up the long battle against pain and permanent disability without his example. The response he got back gave him the strength to keep his jigsaw legs pounding round in unscheduled exercise sessions on the anchored bicycle, suffering agonising pain made more excruciating because it was self-inflicted.

Graham had a poker player's face. A long, fleshy face without being fat. When he wanted to lock himself behind his impregnable bastions he dropped a portcullis that blocked all expression. Even his eyes became less expressive. His wife, Bette, was aware of his agony only by analysing his behaviour before and after the accident and deducing the reason for the change.

Graham had pecked around the periphery of television before the accident. He had even given a splendid portrayal of one of Asimov's less versatile androids in Frankenheimer's film *Grand Prix*, but it was in the winter of '69-'70 that he straightened his tie, powdered his nose and launched himself as a TV personality.

The end of the decade was the end of an era for motor racing. It entered the '70s as a market-researched, glamour-conscious, ready-packaged product that had to sell to exist, and Graham Hill, the product of the '50s, was the only one around capable of epitomising the public's idea of what a racing driver should be.

Left *'It will be transcribed and used in evidence against you.'*

Chapter 2

In for a quid

For anyone who didn't live through the social and economic austerity of the '50s it is hard to imagine what it was like. In spite of the democratising influence of the Second World War and the morale-shattering effect of losing an empire, society was still structured to a stern Victorian ethic; work was good! It was the only discipline capable of keeping the working classes out of the mischief that their dull brains and ox-like bodies would find if they weren't kept securely padlocked to the workbench and plough. Even the recently ripened Labour Party politician in power, sounded and looked more like his standard, wing-collared, pre-war counterpart than his proletarian claims suggested. There were a few exceptions, like Ernie Bevin and Aneurin Bevan. They did the shouting and turned in a good line in finger-stabbing rhetoric but behind them were the ascetic, school teacher gurus like Clement Attlee, Sir Stafford Cripps and John Strachey.

The reinstatement of the Tory Party did little to lighten the nation's spirit. The front benches were inhabited by stalwarts of the 'old school' system with a vested interest in mending the torn fabric of their fine-tapestried society caused by the uneducated masses' disturbing capacity to interpret the printed page and their sudden interest in social questions.

Before the 'flower-power' revolution of the '60s a 'good job' was the best a state educated boy could hope for or reasonably expect, and that was determined very carefully by class, tempered slightly by natural or academic ability. Top of the tree was the Civil Service. If someone got into the black jacket and pin-striped trouser brigade it was a matter of pride for the parents, who could then boast about his pension and the inevitable bungalow near Pinner or Gants Hill. Each type of employment carried its own privilege and stigma. Caught by the drag-anchor of accent it was unlikely for a working-class boy from Bethnel Green to rise higher than a postal clerk or messenger on the Stock Exchange and impossible to get a metal toecap over the polished copper step of an accounting bank, so many drifted into dead-end labouring jobs or the less fastidious end of the service industries.

Cutting against the gravitation back to the staid pre-war world was National Service, a much-maligned institution which brought character and a new sense of independence to those who were willing and able to accept and work the system. Graham Hill was one who could take it and wrestle it into an acceptable shape.

Above left *Graham in a well-worn demob suit and Bette in a classical '50s outfit pose stiffly for the camera.*

Above right *Out of the boiler room and posing with the big guns.*

Below *HMS* Swiftsure, *home to PO Hill.*

By the time he came back on to Civvy Street he knew that there was something out there beside the wage packet, two weeks' paid holiday, the miserly pension that was still dangled before employees like a carrot and the regulation plot in the cemetry with the Funeral Club headstone. It was hard to launch into anything that wasn't an approved occupation and Graham Hill settled into Smiths Clocks with the grace of a gorilla at a coffee morning. The rowing club helped. It was a little above his genealogically defined class but the rank of Petty Officer Artificer had broadened Hill's expectations and he was a good line-shooter and able to hold his own with the 'Blues' and the *aficionadoes*. But that long, dark tube still stretched out before him with the comfortless pension at the end. He needed to break away and find something that would make his tall stories and idle boasting amount to something.

Motor racing wasn't apparently one of the lines on his palm. In fact, motor racing wasn't something that a boy from a normal, lower-incomed family would even think about. It was an upper class sport; all hairy tweed jackets and breeches, bow ties and brogues, an extension of Ascot and Cowes. It was not quite approved of by the aristocrats but indulged because of the element of danger which purifies non-utilitarian pursuits. But the kudos of rowing had begun to diminish. Whatever happened he was going to have to share the glory with seven others and it was a strictly amateur sport where money wasn't even remotely regarded as an incentive. On top of that it was uncomfortable and time-consuming. Evening classes seemed to pave a way forward and Graham enrolled

Left *The invitation to Graham's first visit to Monaco aboard HMS Swiftsure in 1951.*

Right *The ties have it! In Ghent, with the Auriol Rowing Club in May 1950.*

Below *The sport you do backwards sitting down. Semi-finals at Henley, 1953; Graham at no 4.*

for a few courses but could see them leading to only more of what he already had, without proving a balm to his itch to do 'something'.

In the mid-'50s cars came into the picture. Before the war they had been a status symbol that few could afford. Suddenly everyone seemed to be on the road. Cars laid up at the beginning of the war were dusted off and eased out on to the tarmacadam. The biggest boost to four-wheeled society was the release of thousands of ex-WD staff cars and vans. To stay in the swim Graham bought a battered Morris 8 and took to the road. His engineering expertise now had an outlet and he began to take an interest in making his car mechanically more efficient. This led him to the motoring magazines, which were having a field day as the new brand of 'autoholism' gripped a nation struggling to forget the ration book and bomb-site mentality which it had adopted over the years. It was natural that Graham should glance at the brief reports on motor racing sandwiched in between articles on adapting Bedford 15 cwt exhaust pipes for Ford 10s and how to repair the canvas top of a Bulldog Morris with four, easily obtainable canvas kitbags. His interest quickened when he came across a small advertisement in *Autocar* offering four laps of the track at Brands Hatch in a lashed up Formula 500 for 20/-.

The Brands circuit of 1953 had little in common with today's tailored corners and ironed out surface. It began life as a playground for motor bikes, at the back of a farm house. Over the years it established a reputation as a motocross venue and then made a slow suspicious conversion to cars. The paddock was no more than a slab of uneven tarmac and concrete perched muddily on a 1 in 6 hill, while the pits had the appearance of pig-pens erected by students working with breezeblocks and poor quality cement. But that was motor racing and you lumped it or went horse racing.

Having scraped together the 20/-, Graham made a date with Brands Hatch circuit. He prepared his day carefully by claiming a cold and, when his father was safely out of the way, set off for Kent. Four laps and 20/- later he was sure of one thing: the owner of the Universal Motor Racing Club was desperately in need of a mechanic. Graham spoke to the proprietor and filled him in about his extensive knowledge of engineering from instrumentation right through to turbines. He didn't feel called upon to mention that the turbines had been in a ship and the instrumentation was mainly in Smith's alarm clocks. In desperate need of a miracle, and willing to believe anything which might come between his failing business and the broker's man, the proprietor forced himself to believe that the skinny, jut-jawed mechanic might be the sorcerer who could find the alchemist's stone for him. For a few months Graham happily trundled across to Brands in the evenings and at weekends to work on the stock of the Universal Motor Racing Club.

Then one day he arrived and everything had disappeared. The harsh realities of economic life had finally caught up with Universal and Graham was left with his dream in tatters. There wasn't much he could do about it. He had learned a little about racing cars and test-driven a number of laps around the circuit. But he learned considerably more about the desire to get out from under. He drifted back to London Rowing Club and stepped up his socialising. But the locking-tie had been loosened.

His job at Smiths weighed him down more each day. He even had thoughts of returning to the sea or emigrating with his brother Brian to Canada. Anything to feel that he was different, that he didn't need to conform to the pattern forced on him by birth.

Then, as these things have a habit of doing to those open and ready, a conversation in a pub in Paddington brought on new excitement and the conviction that his hour had arrived. Gordon Jones was about to start a racing school and was looking for someone to help out—for free of course! Graham closed his mind to the financial aspect. That could be worked out somehow. The important thing was to get the chance. It meant leaving his job and his only money source but there was always the dole. It was little in actual pounds, shillings and pence and long on stigma but that didn't matter. Cautiously Graham established the details of the job. There would be two Formula 3 cars and he would look after their mechanical welfare. In exchange he would be allowed to race them occasionally and, if successful, to graduate to instructor.

The bargain struck, Hill floated on a fleecy cloud as he severed his connection with the Smiths pension fund and signed on at the Labour Exchange as an out-of-work racing driver—a category which did not require a large space in the filing system. Viewed against the background of daily drudgery, the 32/6 (£1.62½) on tap looked more than enough to keep him going until he had put the grandly

Below left *Brother Brian in Vancouver, where he emigrated in 1955.*

Below right *A blazer, a dashing 'tache and a soon-to-be-world-famous rowing cap. Ted (Bags) Paine and Graham enjoy a 'half' at Henley in 1954.*

named Premier Motor Racing Club on its feet. His only real worry was his father's reaction. Graham had broken one of the prime rules of lower-middle-class society. He had acted unpredictably. The problem of his father was side-stepped temporarily by not telling him what he had done. It was impossible to keep the secret from his mother but sportingly she kept quiet and carefully avoided any conversation which might have led to disclosure.

As the weeks went by, it became obvious that the Premier connection was anything but! What was the good of being able to drop gems from the world of motor racing into the pools of rowing club conversation if financial considerations made it politic to keep on the move to avoid the sticky situation of having to buy a round of drinks? However, Graham revelled in the modest reputation he was acquiring as a forceful, if inelegant, driver and driving instructor, a reputation which could only be enhanced by success on the race circuit. He could easily overlook the lack of financial benefit if his status in motor racing circles was enhanced.

Unfortunately the machinery wasn't up to it. The final straw came when the engine died after a few laps in the biggest race that he had so far managed to enter. Furious at being sidelined, he stormed off into the paddock. As he wandered moodily around he noticed a transporter being loaded up ready to leave. Overseeing the handling was a shortish, energetic man with wavy light brown hair. Graham knew him by sight. He was getting a bit of a reputation for patching together various components and making them work. His name was Colin Chapman. Ever conscious of the sound of opportunity knocking, however faintly, Graham lent a hand and then struck up a conversation. He was looking for a lift back to London and as there was plenty of room in the transporter he soon found himself outside a dilapidated stable in Hornsey. The car on the transporter was a bit bent. As it was pushed into the garage Graham heard the sound of distant knocking again and offered to help straighten it out. Working through the night on the car, Graham Hill and Colin Chapman built up a rapport

Left *Transformation! Graham applied his technical finesse to turning the tatty Austin 7 on the left into the neat job on the right.*

Right *Still rowing orientated, Graham and Bette live it up at Christmas, 1955.*

Below *Colin Chapman was a handy driver himself, both before and while he was busy designing and manufacturing racing cars. In the last race of the season at Brands Hatch, he won the 1200 cc class in one of his own Lotus cars.*

which was to last, with many cuts and diversions, for 20 years and cover a period when British motor racing rose from being a joke and the object of sympathy to being the leading trackside force in international motor racing.

Colin Chapman was not the easiest man to get along with. Graham's first introduction to the international scene with the fast-improving Lotus team was by no means an idyll of two stalwart friends marching shoulder to shoulder, grim-faced and determined, into a schoolboy's dream. There was a tacit understanding that he would get a drive now and then but basically it was his mechanical skill and his strength which were his main assets, and his determination to stay the course whatever the cost. Even when it became a fact that Graham could be expected to negotiate a circuit with a fair degree of accuracy, Chapman was inclined to treat it as a whim that he would grow out of sooner or later. Graham tried to change Chapman's mind—not the easiest of propositions when he had the kind of single-mindedness that revolved around 'I think it—so it must be so!'

Already the Press, always ready to use a handy superlative, were acclaiming the

Lotus boss as a 'genius'. The burgeoning ambitions of master and man were not easily resolved. Ignoring homespun worker relations, 'Chunky' Chapman preferred to buy his headlines with already blooded drivers. His main interest, naturally, was to promote Lotus into the winners' frame. It was a vast ambition, as a British car had never even come within brake-failure distance of a world championship at that point, and the thought of it was enough to bring a weak smile to the *duce* face of the Ferrari head man Enzo. Although Chapman was convinced that his flimsy car would ultimately come through for him, the less committed money went on the Raymond Mays-blessed BRMs. They were anachronistic in comparison with what Lotus was doing but their tank-like structure supported a carefully cossetted engine which was finishing races—a prerequisite for any team. Raymond Mays, still a recognised rester on recent laurels, liked the cut of the Hill jib and was willing to have him aboard.

Graham let Colin know what was going on, still hopeful that he might change spanner for hammer. Chapman affected not to care—after all, there were plenty of mechanics about. Graham swapped cars and gradually the BRM team began to get it together.

By 1962 they were so together that Hill took the Formula 1 World Championship, not without a few nerve-tweaking moments along the way, but with the finishing places on the board it was no time to quibble. For a while Graham seemed confused, it was what he had wanted more than anything and at last he had it—that was what he told himself. But the truth was, that in spite of his vociferous self-assurance, he couldn't find the confidence to believe he was now edging into the frame containing Mike Hawthorn, Fangio, Nuvalari and other celebrated drivers.

Race drivers are often compared to hysterical death-defying hyped-up public school boys from a bygone era. Maybe there is a death wish buried under the Nomex long johns and the encapsulated head. But if there is, it's pretty well submerged under a healthy fear of injury, and, in most adrenalin-charged drivers, a low pain threshold. Probably, after the war, there was still enough of the 'tally-ho' mentality amongst drivers to fill a grid. But they weren't the vintage years of motor racing and it took ten years to start to weed out the 'wizard prang' racers. Mike Hawthorn gave the era a fitting finale by taking the hotly-disputed title from the flag-bearer of the new generation, Stirling Moss. Graham had fought his way through the ranks under the patronage of the lineage drivers. They were his pattern, and their position was his goal, a goal that seemed to disappear the closer he got to it. It left him isolated like a fly trapped in amber. However he wasn't really out of time, since his slightly anachronistic persona was to be one of his strengths in the coming years.

The years between his first world championship, in 1962, and his second world championship, in 1968, were frustrating. Always, the golden chalice seemed to be just out of reach. Race after race, Jimmy Clark pressed home his advantage in the light-weight Lotus thoroughbred that Colin Chapman had at last produced. Hill tried to be blasé about his bridesmaid position but underneath he fumed. The BRM's durability was no match for the more aerodynamically efficient Lotus.

Above *The French Grand Prix of 1962 was held at Rouen. The 1½ litre V8 BRM didn't function well and Graham finished in penultimate place — but he did win the world championship that year.*

Below *Damon gives the BRM the smile of approval.*

Tony Rudd, BRM team manager, gets a few words of advice about setting up a car while Graham waits to benefit from the knowledge — and just to make sure he's got it right he asks about driving technique.

It was about this time, in the mid-'60s, that I first met Graham. He had presented the cheques to the drivers nominated by the Guild of Motoring writers as 'up and coming'. It was while I still had hopes of developing a career as a racing driver and so I made sure that I stuck near him when the crowds had melted away and dinner was being discussed. It's the sycophant's conviction that if he stays with the loudest buzzing bees, an extra dollop of honey can be cornered. How this could possibly be effective is a little obscure but the conviction is hard to kill. The final choice of venue, not unexpectedly, was the Steering Wheel Club, not the brass-knockered upstairs rooms sharing Shepherds Market with other less solubrious establishments, but the more restricted quarters in Brick Street. A table was hastily laid for us in a corner and I made sure I got a seat next to the World Champion, convinced that my rather dog-eared Anglia would benefit from the reflected aura and produce something really startling at Snetterton the next weekend.

It was a good evening. Graham, in great form, told blue jokes and sang blue songs until well after the time when the waiters, obtrusively switching off lights and banging furniture, thought them funny. I made sure that I laughed loudest and harmonised the most melodiously in my effort to grab some of the magic.

Happily, Graham didn't seem to notice. He was having a good time and that was enough for him. It wasn't enough for me. Driving home in the early hours of the morning my head was full of the startling career possibilities my new intimacy with the World Champion was going to foster. It was going to be the

entrée into a world where trade sponsors would cluster around desperately pushing their wares in an effort to curry favour with the World Champion's friend.

The euphoria was still there a couple of days later when I set off to get a few laps' practice at Snetterton. Just outside Harlow I picked up a couple of American students hitch-hiking around Britain. I didn't need much encouragement to launch into my motor racing tales. The two young Americans confessed to knowing a little about the sport and seemed to think it included the Indianapolis 500 and many other class events, organised as carnivals in the States and involving unwieldy cars with giant, inefficient engines. My sympathetic smile showed them the error of their thinking. (It was before Jimmy Clark and Graham Hill had taken the Brickyard apart and given it respectability, and a long time before Denny Hulme and the McLarens were going to prove big was beautiful in the Can Am races.)

By the time we reached Thetford they had somehow got the impression that Graham owed his racing career to me and that only modesty and good sportsmanship stopped me from going out on the circuit and giving him a salutary lesson. And, of course, I couldn't leave it alone. That's the problem when you find a good audience. It's easy to go over the top. When we arrived at the circuit I just had to invite them in. They declined at first but I was beginning to believe my own publicity and made a refusal practically an international affront. As I drove along the decaying concrete slabs towards the decayed concrete pits I began to have doubts about depositing my innocents amongst a group of *aficionados* whose view of my racing career might not coincide in detail with my rather free interpretation. The situation became even less rosy when, judging from the fact that the huge BRM transporter was standing in the paddock, it became obvious that the Grand Prix team was testing at Snetterton that day. There was nothing to do but brazen it out.

The BRM team was sorting something out and Graham was sitting in a chair, his Nomex overall peeled off to the waist, feet resting on the Armco barrier while the mechanics prodded around the entrails of his car. After carefully directing my guests to a pit as far away as possible, I wheeled the Anglia around and began giving it an inexperienced once over in an effort to prevent some of the least secure parts from spreading themselves around the circuit. A shadow fell across the engine and a head craned under the bonnet. When I saw who it was my jaw dropped into the fan belt. 'How is it going?' Graham asked, solicitously eyeing the trembling 998 cc engine. I nodded energetically, not trusting my engine enough to voice an opinion. Quickly my eyes shot across to the two Americans watching with wide-eyed interest. Obviously their restricted motoring education stretched to the World Champion. It gave me encouragement, so I made wild, expansive gestures and explained some of the intricacies of the Anglia until he found he couldn't absorb any more and wandered back to his chair. At that moment I knew I had the stuff that world champions were made of. Half an hour later, out on the track, I wasn't so sure. Every time I went into a corner there was a BRM in the mirror with Graham waving wildly at me, and he wasn't just being friendly. Next time I went into the pits the marshal came over and became very unpleasant. And Graham didn't say good-bye to me when he left.

Chapter 3

A major rebuild

The Watkins Glen accident in 1969 marked a change in tempo. When Graham came out of University College Hospital it was in a blaze of publicity. While this was very satisfying to the Hill ego it had a draw-back. The millions who had become aware of his dogged fight for limited mobility wanted a finale—a capper to the stories of unrelenting exercise and non-stop physiotherapeutic treatment that had made column inches around the world. Come what may, Graham had to be in his car, fit for the South African Grand Prix at Kyalami in 1970, even if it meant lifting him in and working him by radio control.

However, there was a problem. Colin Chapman was not happy about having Graham back in the Lotus team and had promised Jochen Rindt that efforts in 1970 were going to be devoted to making him top dog. To avoid having two Number Ones he intended to back Rindt with John Miles. Now, with Graham forcing himself back to fitness, it looked as if Chapman might have to face the notoriously short tempered Austrian with the news that they had a problem.

The solution he found saved face all round. Rob Walker, a leading personality in motor racing since the pre-war days when men were men and seat belts weren't invented, agreed to run a Lotus, with Brooke Bond tea sponsorship and factory help, for the return of the grizzled warrior. The deal had already been talked about the previous year and was hastily put back on the flame. The acrimony over Chapman's two-foot shuffle was kept strictly under wraps and thin smiles plastered over the cracks in public bonhomie. Graham had his chariot tweaked up and ready to go for the South African Grand Prix. The query was whether the charioteer could apply the whip with the accuracy and dexterity of yore.

Graham rose to the occasion magnificently. Seemingly unaware of the attention he was attracting he limped, without a single grimace of pain, the length of the pit lane and carefully threaded his stiff body down behind the steering wheel. The world's photographers, who had waited for this moment, were disappointed that they hadn't captured a wince or a wry look of suffering subdued. It was just as Hill intended. He was too instinctive a player to force the game. There were plenty of people around to point up his performance without underscoring every move he made. Mr. Twikey, the surgeon responsible for putting Hill together again, was there, shaking his head and disclaiming responsibility for anything which might go wrong with the network of scar-tissue, plates and pins. And there

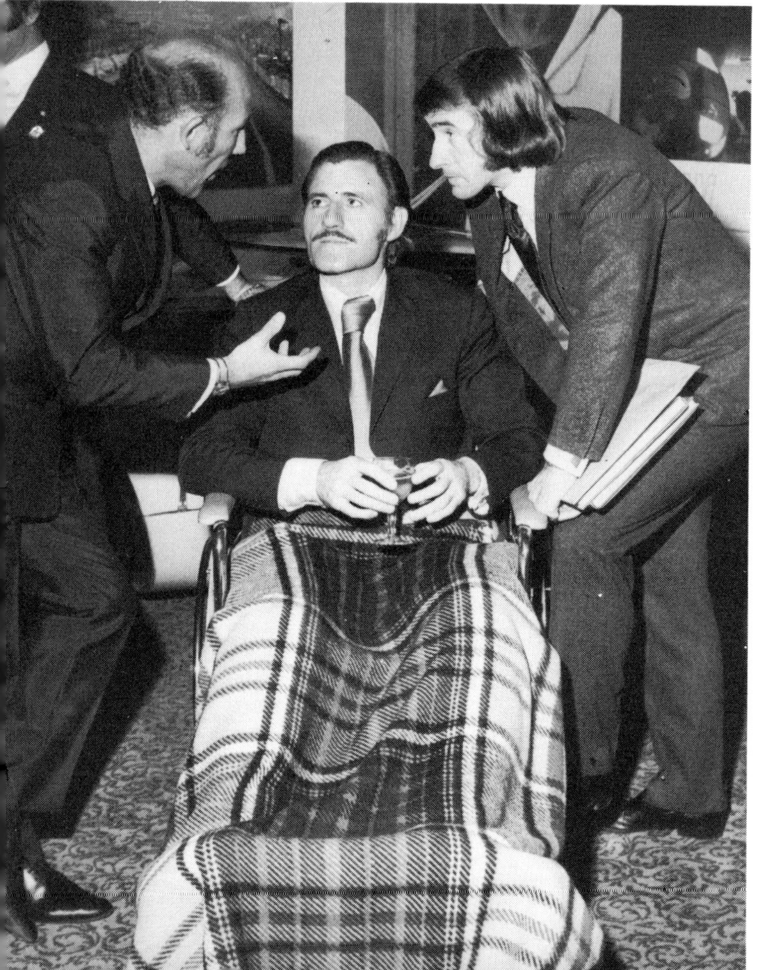

Above In the University College
Hospital after the operation to put
his legs back together again following the Watkins Glen accident in
1969.

Left Stirling Moss and Jackie
Stewart arguing over who should
push Graham's wheelchair at the
Ferodo Trophy presentation to
John Wyer in 1969.

Right Graham made the switch
from the official Lotus team to the
Brooke Bond/Oxo, Rob Walker
Team for 1970, and drove the
Lotus 49c.

was Rob Walker, an experienced team manager in the old tradition, making protective movements like a mother hen at incubation time.

The first practice session was hell. Severed nerves in Graham's legs made sensitive manipulation of the pedals impossible and he had to thrust down with his feet and hope. Incredibly he came through this session unscathed. Now the pressure showed. Knowing heads nodded as Graham's exhausted body was lifted from his torture chamber and reverently laid on a pile of tyres and overalls in the corner of the pit garage. Sensing the chance to get the picture they had been denied earlier, the Press surged back, but they weren't to get what they wanted. Even the hard-bitten team mechanics were impressed by Hill's incredible performance, and, led by a less-than-debonair Rob Walker, kept the eager shutter-snappers at bay until the exhausted driver had recovered enough to face them.

Around the pool at the picturesque Kyalami Ranch, a collection of westernised Kraal-type, thatched native huts with all mod-cons, it was generally agreed that Hill had done his bit and stuck two firm fingers up at those who said he would never make it back. Now was the time to withdraw gracefully. The organisers, not untypically, were not so sensitive. Their days of glory were short-lived and they intended to get full value. After half-hearted enquiries about his health, they dragged him off to a dinner party organised by the Wanderer's Club where Graham managed to put on a typically bravura show, in spite of pain and fatigue that gouged deep black pits around his eyes.

Everybody was surprised when he arrived at the circuit the following morning. As he eased himself creakily out of the Range Rover, a crowd of fans moved in. Graham straightened and dug deep for a tight-lipped smile. Noticeable was the absence of the Press. Most of them were still at the Ranch, lolling around the pool and eyeing the lovely girls inevitably attracted to the lair of the racing drivers. Those who had ventured onto the tarmac in the hot morning sun weren't worried about getting a snap of the ex-World Champion's token appearance. The only shot they wanted was the one where, after a lap or two, he would pull into the pits and be persuaded, by team manager Rob Walker, to make a judicious withdrawal from the ranks. The scenario had already been written by the hacks. Only the time was still to be decided. As Friday progressed and there was no apparent move by the Walker equipe to throw in the towel, schedules were

revised. Obviously Hill was going to struggle through practice and then make a big thing of withdrawing from the race and permanently retiring just before the start on Saturday. That way he would grab the headlines and not have to race. Nothing was further from Graham Hill's mind. By now he was hardly mentally balanced. The pain and singleminded determination had become a narrow tunnel with an enticing light at the end.

Last thing on the night before a race, whenever practical, Graham would make a final visit to the garage to see how his car was coming along. It was part of the charade that he made his tour of inspection that night. Anyone seeing him chatting to the mechanics would never have guessed that he had hardly had the strength to get up off the bed after the rest he had taken following dinner. Untimed practice next morning was half an hour. Wisely Graham conserved his strength by only making a couple of slow, testing laps before retiring to a low, reclining armchair fixed up at the back of his pit garage by the mechanics. The mechanics, usually the most placid and agreeable people at a race circuit, were like snarling dogs jealously guarding a prize hunk of brisket that morning. The few journalists and unwelcome well-wishers who tried to slip through the little wicket gate were bundled out unceremoniously. Of all the people there, they, the mechanics, knew most the tremendous guts their driver was showing and they had no intention of letting anyone disturb him.

On the start line the Brooke Bond car didn't look too potent. It was at the back of the grid. Driving on adrenalin and experience but practically no tactile reference from his legs, Hill remorselessly forced himself on. To everyone's astonishment the Hill Lotus kept going and finished in a sensational sixth spot. This championship point was the sweetest Graham had ever earned, and, for valour beyond the call of reason, earns him a place beside Niki Lauda when awards are handed out.

The Press had their moment but now began to lose interest. There are just so many superlatives you can use and then it's time to move on. At first Graham was too preoccupied with getting a few degrees more co-operation from his lower limbs. Golf was a solace. Before the accident he had sliced a few balls into the rough on an *ad hoc* basis. Told to do the thing he had dreaded all his life—walk—he now turned to golf as a way to make it tolerable. It wasn't a mellow union. Graham studied the mechanics of swinging a 4 sq ins flange of metal on a 3 ft stick at a 1.32 ins ball and proceeded to drive deeper and deeper into the rough. Lessons with the golfers' 'pro', John Jacobs, only told him what he knew already—he had to overcome the natural strength in his arms and swing the clubhead. Hill gritted his teeth and spent a long time addressing the ball but without really getting his message across. That's not to say he didn't enjoy it. His half dozen clubs and sawn-off putter had a permanent place in the luggage compartment of his Aztec Turbo D wherever he went. Every week he tried to get at least one game in, either at the Mill Hill Golf Club where he was a member, or anywhere else that he fancied. He was even instrumental in forming a golfing society called FIDASHOGS (Formula One Drivers and Sundry Hangers On Golf Society).

Above *True-blue Brit Rob Walker and Graham had a close relationship going back over the years and Rob was able to help the World Champion in his battle to get well.*

Below *Lotus 49c takes a tight line around Tarzan in the 1970 Dutch Grand Prix at Zandvoort.*

At Formula 2 meetings, where the pressure was less intense than in Grand Prix racing, it was a toss up at times which interested him most—the racing or the prospect of a game of golf.

Rouen was one meeting where the emphasis finally came down on golf. The Saturday evening before the race Graham had been playing at the Rouen Golf Club and decided to walk back to the Hotel de la Poste where all the teams stayed. To make it more interesting he putted the ball along the road, with an occasional chip on the grassier bits, until he got to the hotel. The hotel, although in the middle of Rouen, has a small forecourt and an imposing entrance at the top of a flight of stone stairs. While Grahame White, at that time General Manager of the BARC (British Automobile Racing Club), obligingly held the swing-doors open, Hill selected a 9 iron and tried to hole out in the lobby. A slight error of judgement, or maybe an imbalance in the ball, angled it across the courtyard and smashed one of the mullioned windows at the side. He wasn't very popular with the management.

Next day his appetite for punishing the little white ball had not abated. The car he was driving, a Rondel Brabham BT 36, wasn't inspiring much confidence, and most of the practice session had been spent in the pits. The race was in two

Reassuringly Rob Walker remains impassive while Graham seems a little doubtful about the state of the car.

heats and a final. Graham reckoned that there was no way that he was even going to get through the heat, let alone get into the final. Plans were laid to make tracks to the golf course as soon as his car dropped out, which, on it's practice showing, should be shortly after the start. Alas, he finished in third position and got into the final. But all was not lost. He was sure that the car could not possibly last the course so there would be a chance of getting away before the crowd and still get 18 holes in before dark. He finished third in the final! This meant he had to go to the prize giving.

At most Formula 2 meetings this is little more than a perfunctory slap on the back in the Goodyear trailer and then everyone dives off with their silverware to do battle with the crowd; but not this time! There was to be a ceremonial laying on of hands at a local château with *le maire* and his entourage in attendance. Hill was equal to the delay. Now the plan was that a car should be standing by, Graham would shake the appropriate hands, swill a mandatory glass of bubbly, grab the trophy and run. It didn't quite work out like that. The French love the chance to orate and *le maire* was no exception. But at last he dried up and Hill did a swift bunk.

Getting out of Rouen on race day is a bit like getting over Twickenham Bridge

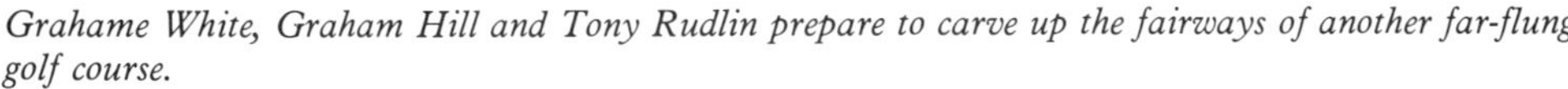

Grahame White, Graham Hill and Tony Rudlin prepare to carve up the fairways of another far-flung golf course.

when England is playing Wales. Solid traffic hooted and steamed through the town and over the bridges. Golf looked like taking second best to getting to the hotel in time for breakfast, except that Graham had now firmly fixed in his mind his determination to try out his latest theory on how he was going to break through the 24 handicap barrier. Thinking laterally, he avoided the crowded road and took to the pavement. This was equally crowded but pedestrians are more agile and can react quicker when they see a car bearing down on them. Scowls soon turned to sycophantic smiles and waves when the marauder was recognised, and few people were willing to disapprove openly of his cavalier action; until he got to the crossroads! One of those big gendarmes, in the scuffed leathers and jack-boots, who usually hide on the blind side of a bend with double yellow lines, was venting his spleen on motorists daring to keep him away from his pleasures. When he saw Hill's car surging along the pavement he nearly swallowed his whistle. Screaming, his face a deep mottled red, his whistle shrilling so loudly it threatened to disintegrate the pea, he threw himself in the car's path and slammed gauntletted hands down with panel-buckling force on the bonnet. It looked for a moment as if even the cultivated Hill charm was not going to be balm enough to get him out of this. As the huge gendarme lunged towards the driver, Graham popped his head through the window and gave a toothpaste smile. Awestruck, the cop stopped short and snatched his whistle guiltily from his mouth like a naughty schoolboy. 'Grehem Eel . . .' he said in a hushed tone. Graham knew he had it made. He stuck out a hand, shook the shaken policeman by the gauntlet and followed up with a Lotus badge. Lotus badges have for many years been the standard currency for bribing gatemen, garage owners, and policemen. It worked spectacularly this time. The stirred gendarme leaped officiously back into the maelstrom of homebound traffic and gave a virtuoso performance on his whistle while at the same time exhibiting manual dexterity that would not have shamed a giant squid. In the fading light, at the eighteenth hole, Graham reflected that none of his golfing theories could exorcise a golf ball's fear of falling into little dark holes.

Chapter 4

The Murphy factor

An activity which helped to keep Graham's mind occupied and stop him facing facts was flying. Along with others of the motor racing jet set, Hill had opted out of the Mile High Club in favour of taking to the air in the left hand seat. At first it was more or less to be in with the boys. If Colin Chapman and Jimmy Clark could do it, why shouldn't he? Later it got more serious and the possibility of flying to races under his own propeller power became more alluring. Swanning around Europe in blue skies was one thing. Trying to maintain some sort of believable schedule in nil visibility was ambition on a different flight level. It meant getting an Instrument Rating, which is not the easiest thing to do when you're dashing around all over the place trying to keep ahead in the popularity poll. When he was confined to his bed in the University College Hospital he had tried to get to grips with a correspondence course supplied by the Commercial School of Flying at Oxford. It was not an appropriate time to try and memorise pages of jargon and rules, when the prospect loomed large that the most powerful crate he might pilot for the rest of his life was an electric wheelchair. As soon as he could make the break with the doctors and physiotherapists he whipped across the Atlantic to do a condensed course at ATE (Aviation Training Enterprises) in New York. It wasn't difficult. He already had a good deal of instrument flying experience. The piece of paper he got at the end of the course made it legal. Europe opened up to him and his flying and golf acted as counter balance to the fear that his racing career wasn't going as well as he would have liked. The knowledge that, as Mary Peters injudiciously quipped on the BBC Sportsman of the Year show, he might be over the hill did not settle lightly on the Hill ego.

Always a perfectionist, he now tried to compensate for the bluntness that age brought to his reflexes by blaming his car. Preparing for a race became a battle of wills between driver and mechanic. Never an easy man to work for, he nevertheless retained the respect of his mechanics. Like a tailor, the mechanics have a relationship with the client which far exceeds the obvious. The tailor knows that he must cut the trousers so that tears don't appear in his customer's eyes every time he crosses his legs. The mechanic is aware that the drivers' life is literally in his hands every time he ventures out on to the track. Knowing this, the mechanic has a hard time. When a driver goes flat into a corner, braking and accelerating, he is giving a collossal vote of confidence to his mechanics and designer. If something goes wrong, it's too late for the man in the pit to think of

Graham was suitably impressed with the cockpit of Concord when he was shown over it by Brian Trubshaw.

the locking wire he should have put on or the nut he should have tightened. To him the car represents the pinnacle of his art. Racing the car only has merit in that it proves to the other engineers that he can prepare a car to the ultimate degree of efficiency. When a mechanic finds that his driver is looking for his lost ability in his car, the respect disappears. That's not how it should work. The car is prepared to the best of the mechanic's ability and he expects the driver to appreciate that and reciprocate with driving of an equal standard.

It was about this time that Graham became vocal about 'perfection' and 'luck'. The quest was for perfection unaided by luck, which does not exist. Luck was merely something to throw into an equation when facts couldn't be quantified. Graham claimed that 'luck' was not an appropriate word to use around motor racing stables. What you did was define the areas. There were areas where you had good solid facts, or at least as near as you could get to good solid facts. These areas seemed to be somewhat restricted. A car had four wheels, an all-up weight, a defined engine capacity developing a guesstimate brake horsepower and a length of track that ran for so many miles—more or less. The rest was not so well substantiated. Graham claimed that to eliminate luck it was now necessary to do the best with the parts that there was some measure of control over, and leave the rest to the Murphy factor—a brave theory and one hotly pursued by Hoyle but not an easy one to nail down.

The result was that Graham spent more and more time probing around under the bonnet, metaphorically, and less and less time behind the wheel on the track proving the car's capabilities. Not that he wasn't having success. Considering his physical condition and the mental hazard that has to be negotiated after any bad accident, he was doing more than anyone expected. The thing that bugged everyone was whether or not it was necessary.

Remembered for his rugged determination and double world championship, surely Graham would bow out gracefully?

Television had at last caught up with him and he was being pushed further into the spotlight. There seemed no more reason for him to force his patched up body to try to prove the unprovable. Those daring enough to ask him about retirement were initially met with the pert reply that when he thought of something better to do on Sunday afternoons he would hang up his helmet. But the question kept being asked and its implication was that Hill should retire. On top of this there was Chapman's unwillingness to have him in the official Lotus team, and so the question began to sting.

With the notable exception of his fantastic sixth place at Kyalami, the year after his accident, 1970, wasn't good by anyone's reckoning, especially not Hill's and those who rated him higher than a has-been hanging on for the last vainglorious curtain call. Points in the driver's championship from four races, South Africa, Spain, Monaco and Great Britain, raised him no higher than thirteenth in the table. It was a bad year all round. McLaren was killed in a testing accident. Piers Courage had run out of road at Zandvoort and died in a magnesium fire of horrific proportions and Jochen Rindt had perished in practice at Monza when his car had gone straight on at the Parabolica. By the time the Lotus succumbed in the 1970 Mexican Grand Prix, the last race of the season, with an overheating engine, its driver had built up a good head of steam. The year that had started so well had dribbled away into nothing. The following year Graham was determined that it was all going to be different.

The Brabham 'Lobster Claw' at Silverstone, March 1971.

Millionaire chemist and second-hand car salesman Bernie Ecclestone had bought the Brabham equipe and was now looking for an ace development driver to make the exciting new 'lobster claw' Brabham BT 34 work. Ron Tauranac, Bernie's partner and ex-owner of the Brabham team, set a lot of store by the BT 34. Although he was grateful to Rob Walker for giving him the opportunity to race in the 1970 season, Graham felt it was time to move on. He was 41 and not getting any younger, and so he joined the Brabham team.

When the BT 34 didn't start taking the circuits apart at the beginning of the 1971 season he didn't mind too much. It was obvious that it was going to take a bit of time, a race or two at least, to get it together. Anyway, he had confidence in his team. Bernie Ecclestone, at this time just another team owner with big ideas and far from being the czar of international racing that he is today, was busy bolstering the Hill ego. He told everybody who would listen about the enormous amounts of foreign money he had turned down to keep the Brabham team British. There was going to be no nonsense about joint number one drivers or any of the antics that had marred Graham's time at Lotus. Graham Hill was going to be the 'Primo', with a new car and total back-up.

As a makeweight—'Well, two cars are almost as cheap to run as one'—Tim Schenken, a much fancied Aussie driver, was to get race experience in an outdated BT 33. Even Graham's mechanics were handpicked. Bob Dance, who had been with Graham at Lotus, was brought in as chief mechanic. Filched from McLaren was Kiwi Kerry Adams and an old friend and ex-Grand Prix driver, Keith Green, was in as team manager. All should have been sweetness and light at the

Left *Graham and Bernie Ecclestone discuss the odds at Fordsport Day, Brands Hatch, 1972.*

Right *Graham gets congratulated by Bette after his forceful return to form in the Formula 2 Jochen Rindt Memorial race at Thruxton on Easter Monday 1971.*

collection of mildewed army huts in a copse, known grandly as the 'Brabham Factory'.

Hill did his bit. The Hill/Schenken partnership lapped over into Formula 2 where Motul money had joined with shipping magnate Tony Vlassopulos' investment under the auspices of two ex-Brabham mechanics Neil Trundle and Ron Denis, under the banner of Rondel Racing. In spite of getting nowhere in the South African Grand Prix, and retiring in Spain and Monaco, the Formula 2 results indicated that the 'ole man' might still be able to put together something decisive. Narrowly edged out in a two heat race in Hockenheim by French heart-throb François Cevert, Hill swept aside all opposition a week later to storm home a heady winner in front of his home crowd at Thruxton. The rest of the season didn't match up to the early promise and this, added to a feeling of uneasiness creeping into the Brabham set-up, didn't help re-inflate the flagging team spirit down in the forest.

It started at the top and dripped chillingly down. Ron Tauranac had fallen in with Bernie Ecclestone's plans because he thought the change would leave things exactly as they were. Bernie would loaf around the circuits doing the visiting dignitary act, leaving Ron to get down to the real business of running the team. The reality wasn't working out that way. One reason being that Bernie wasn't going to be a cypher in anyone's manual. Ron, one of the top innovative racing car designers, lacked the phlegm to be a top rank team manager. When Black Jack Brabham had been around he had been able to supply enough phlegm for both of them. Bernie was another kettle of paranoias. Highly strung, he managed to keep

Graham and Ron Tauranac, Brabham boss, standing up and being counted when it was announced at the Hilton that they were joining forces for 1971.

his emotional urges under control by sheer will-power. Quiet-spoken and quick-smiling, with a dry sense of humour, he still proved an irritant that Tauranac couldn't ignore. Caught in the middle was Graham, himself at a cross-roads and unwilling to act as a sounding board for the two contestants.

The manifestly unsuccessful performance of the BT 34 formed a good working foundation for Ecclestone's dry wit and by mid-season he and Tauranac were hardly talking to each other. Graham, knowing a good thing when it paraded in front of him, tended to lean towards the newcomer. The fact wasn't overlooked by the designer. When Hill wanted to play around with the Tauranac design he was tartly told that the car was made to perform in a certain manner and the ex-champion should change his style to suit the car rather than the other way around. This was an injudicious contention! Even Colin Chapman, a well-known zealot where his designs were concerned, had never had the temerity to suggest such a thing.

Jack Oliver, who was a contemporary at Lotus of Jimmy Clark and Graham Hill, on more than one occasion had a chance to drive cars set up for both of the champions. Jimmy was no trouble. He just drove the car as it was made and let his natural ability make up for any inadequacies in design. For Graham it was different. He hadn't Clark's gift and had to work for every success he had. This often required a quite marked changing of the car to suit his style of driving.

What Chapman had tolerated, became a fighting cause for Tauranac and he tried, often unsuccessfully, to make sure that the car on the grid was essentially the car in the workshop.

In spite of this Graham showed remarkable *sang froid*. It seemed as if he was determined to keep everything hermetically sealed while he sorted out what was to be done.

Half way through the 1971 season there was an inaugural Formula 2 race when the new concrete and Scalextric circuit of Paul Ricard opened near Marseilles. The money had been put up by the famous company that bottles the Ricard aperitif and it was launched amid a great hullaballoo which helped to draw attention from the immediate inadequacies of the Micky Mouse circuit. It seemed that the track had been sacrificed to the needs of the Press and visiting dignitaries.

Huge halls were filled with restaurants and telex machines, typewriters and all the paraphernalia of the scribe's art. Even the open Press boxes on the start/finish line were equipped with television sets and closed-circuit earphones. But the track was another matter. Well, it was the first fixture and there was the compensation of the dozens of statuesque, miniskirted hostesses to divert the attention, plus a plethora of Porsche cars handed out to anyone who seemed to have half an excuse for being there.

Graham loved all the attention he got. Even such groupie's delights as Francois Cevert and Derek Bell faded into insignificance beside the debonair Englishman. It was an exhausting weekend. Graham had flown down to the meeting in the Aztec with Bette. On Monday morning he wanted to be away early. As is the common practice in a lot of continental hotels, the management retains passports until the shifty foreigners have paid their bills. Bette didn't discover that the passports were still nestling in the hotel pigeon hole until a friendly customs officer asked to have a peek at them. With one eye on Graham she had to confess that she had forgotten to pick them up in the rush to get away early. Even Bette was surprised when Graham calmly offered to run her back to the hotel to pick them up.

The reason for Graham's state wasn't hard to find. He was like a shipwrecked mariner plucked from the sea at the last moment and given a heroe's welcome. After the dismal showing of 1970 he hadn't really been expecting much of '71. But there he was being fêted and wooed by the press, back in motor racing with a leading team with a chance to show what he could do. Right at the beginning of the year he had been given the doubtful honour of having Eamon Andrews sneak up on him and solemnly inform him, as if he were in doubt, that 'Graham Hill: This is your life!' It was stage-managed at the Hilton Hotel when Graham went to meet the Press for the launch of his reborn career with Brabham. It was a nice gesture but, as with all of these programmes, tended to be over-sentimental and superficial. Then, of course, to add to his Thruxton Formula 2 success there was the Daily Express International Trophy at Silverstone.

GOOD

Background photograph *Hill hedged in by pushy newcomers in the 1971 Spanish Grand Prix in Barcelona's beautiful but infamous Montjuich Park ciruit. Ganley (BRM) leads Hill (BT 34), Schenken (BT 33) and Wissel (Lotus 72).*

Above *Looking for his sixth win at Monaco in 1971, Graham made an unaccustomed error and shunted his BT 34 into the wall at Tabac on his second lap.*

Above *The ubiquitous Eamonn Andrews hits Graham with his big red book at the Brabham reception in the Hilton in 1971.*

Below *Bette, Graham and Eamonn listen to John Coombs doing what's expected on* This is your life.

It seemed like the end of a drought which had started in Watkins Glen with the shunt at the end of 1969 and extended to the time he powered around Woodcote and into the results book. On the back of the trailer on his lap of honour he looked revitalised. He stood with an arm around Bette and drank in the adulation of a crowd genuinely happy to see him back on top again. It was the solid basis of hope laid down in the early months that carried him through the disappointments later. Back in the public eye with a diary filled with dates he felt it was just a matter of holding on and he would be able to give the emaciated character with the scythe a good hobble for his money.

By the end of the year he had begun to change. He didn't grow fangs, or hair on the back of his hands but it was obvious that his ego was being pulled out of shape, and didn't have the ability it had formerly possessed to return to normal. The public homage he was receiving, his country gentleman style of life, friendship with the royal family and his instant gurumanship on TV and in the papers didn't sit easily with the results he was getting on the track.

At the factory the atmosphere darkened and then cleared for a while. The Hill/Ecclestone/Tauranac triangle was resolved by a subtle Ecclestone move which had the former Brabham boss packing his slide-rule in a state of petulance, leaving the field clear for a new broom whose youth, it was hoped, would allow Graham to get his act sorted out without locking horns with anyone. The new man was Gordon Murray, a South African with exciting ideas for the future. 1972 was to be Graham's last year as a pure, unsullied racing driver. Now firmly established in the eyes of a non-motor racing public, it would have been easy to drift gracefully away from the scene and leave it to the younger men, but this was not his style! Besides, there was that ever-present spectre of the day when the bank manager slammed the shutters down on his reaching fingers. Money was pouring into motor racing as if a special mint had been conjured into being just to print notes to spend at circuits. With everything going for him how could he quit now?

Up until that time, Graham's needs outside his sport had been modest. His aeroplane, extravagant by some standards, was not only economically sensible for a man who travelled as much as he did, but almost a necessity. Cars usually ran on the Ford Press Department's budget and there was always a Press man eager to lend him any other car he wanted without any date for return. His home was a comfortable family house on the outskirts of London at Mill Hill. From the outside it could not have been more ordinary, but a peek through the front door soon informed the caller that it was not what it seemed. Everywhere shelves, window sills and niches were loaded with the plunder of the tracks. Hardly an inch of wall was not covered by a picture of Graham or a momento of a race. With three growing children; Brigitte 14, Damon 12 and Samantha 7, it was getting overcrowded.

Bette had been looking around for somewhere to move and she had got Graham to agree that when a suitable place was found they could take it. They found what they were looking for in Shenley, a few miles from Elstree aerodrome and less than 20 miles from London. It wasn't exactly what either of them had had in mind when they decided to move but the idea soon grew on them. 'Lyndhurst' was built in the style of a mid-Victorian country house and was surrounded by parklands. Bette had looked at it a few years earlier but then it had been a big, gloomy hangar of a place, still retaining the atmosphere of the hospital it had previously been. Since then it had been bought by a builder who had completely renovated the whole house. Graham breathed deeply and took on the commitment. It wasn't a matter of rushing into it, finding he was over-committed when he was too far in to withdraw, and in desperation clinging on to the only lifebelt that was likely to see him through. It was more the other way around. He was acting deliberately so that he would have an excuse to continue to lead his life in the manner that made him happy.

The 25 rooms at 'Lyndhurst' gave the Hill family a chance to spread out. They had always loved entertaining, at least Bette had, and now they were able to give bigger and better parties than they ever could in their Mill Hill house, not that Graham got to many of them. He was so heavily committed to a round of public appearances and speaking engagements that he rarely got home until the sparrows were waking up. He had two houses to keep. Down in the wilds of Kent, at Brabourne near Ashford, he had a chocolate box, 17th century timbered cottage which he had leased from Earl Mountbatten. The cottage had been taken as a weekend hideaway to get them away from town. With every weekend a working weekend it wasn't used a lot, except at the time of the British Grand Prix. Then a tent would be erected in the garden and the Grand Prix circus, ringmaster, high wire act and clowns would be invited back for a party that went on all night and the following day, when the race was on Saturday. It was also the home base for the annual cricket match, which was put on with the Grands Prix teams fielding cricketing aces like Emerson Fittipaldi from Brasil, Austria's Niki

Left *The nice family down the road. Outside the house in Mill Hill; Bette, Brigitte, Damon and Graham.*

Above Right *The house in Mill Hill.*

Right *Lyndhurst. On the right, one of David Wynne's sculptures.*

Above left *Damon gives his father a lift to the wicket to save the old boy's legs.*
Above right *Damon Hill seems to be avoiding the necessity of commenting on his father's performance at the crease.*
Right *Colin Chapman dropped in on Carnaby Street on his way to Ashford to advise Graham on the mechanics of striking leather with willow at the annual after the Grand Prix cricket match, 1972.*

Lauda, Jochen Mass from Germany, and stalwarts from many more countries, whose standard reaction to the mention of cricket was to proffer their cigarette lighter. The opposition was known as the Brabourne Team, headed by the son-in-law of Lord Louis, Lord John Brabourne, and encompassing such notables as Prince Charles.

As the 1971 season drew to a close Graham took stock of his position. He still had a year to run on his Brabham contract and with the promise of better things to come in 1972 he should have been happy. The cloud on his horizon was that the Press pundits had decided that it was time for him to retire and a column was incomplete without a reference, humorous or profane, to his age. It chipped away at his shell of confidence and made him even pricklier than his normally short-tempered self. Gradually, a plan formed in his mind, a plan which wouldn't have occurred to him even a year earlier. He would form his own team! Many times he had opined in the past that racing drivers should stick to their steering wheels and not get caught up in the management side. Now he began to revise his ideas. A description that had sprung readily to the pencil and been pushed around by PR men when referring to Graham was 'Ambassador of Sport'. In fact he had become more than just an ambassador in many ways. 'Mr Motor Racing' suited him better because, as his TV appearances multiplied, he came to epitomise the dashing racing driver for the general public.

Left *This is more difficult than racing! Graham Hill batting at the Grand Prix Drivers' Charity Cricket Match, 1972.*

Below *A star-studded if unlikely line-up at the Grand Prix Drivers' Charity Cricket Match, 1974. Back row left to right: Tyrrell, Watson, Edwards, Hailwood, Hunt, Hill, Depailler, Gethin, Purley and Regazzoni. Front row left to right: Scheckter, Bell, Lauda, Stewart, Peterson, Mass and Hulme.*

Cautiously Graham laid the ground work. Without actually committing himself he let the word drop in appropriate places that he might be interested in getting involved more deeply in the game than as one of the up-front hot-shots. His new pairing at Brabham was with Carlos Reutemann from Argentina. Carlos had been around the European circuits for two seasons now and was recognised as a threat to the establishment. An early tendency to stock-car tactics had been replaced by a deadly seriousness. He had no interests or conversation outside motor racing and was looking for the same dedication from those around him. Reutemann was an admirer of Hill, recognising in him many of the qualities that made up his own taciturn character. Both men were thinking drivers, relying on determination and experience to get results, but tending to be overshadowed by more spectacular and natural drivers; Reutemann's sky being clouded by mercurial Swede Ronnie Peterson in Formula 2 and Graham having first Jimmy Clark and then Jackie Stewart getting between him and the sun. With Tauranac sidelined and Ecclestone now in undisputed control, Hill hoped that a good year in Brabham might mean that his fail safe plan of taking on all the headaches of running his own team might not be necessary, then he could just work on his public image safe in the knowledge that his star wouldn't fade as soon as he hung up his helmet.

Again the year started well, not so much on the motor racing front as in the glare of public relations. Hill found himself voted 'Top After Dinner Speaker' by the Guild of Toast Masters. At the first motor race of the season in Buenos Aires in January 1972 he was in sparkling form and the lion of Portenos' society. The Federal Capital of Argentina, renowned for the beauty of its women and the quick temper of its macho men, suited Graham. The hundreds of clustering restaurants purveying high class cuisine at sub-Joe's Cafe prices, with a bottle of top grade wine at 15p and champagne from San Juan at 50p a pop, made it a revellers' paradise. After the gastronomic frolics, finishing usually about 1am, everybody moved, en masse, to the colourful *boites*, refined by a century of good living, which cater for the night-hawk population in a manner befitting a country where the rich are really rich and the poor keep out of the way.

The Argentine Press is colourful to say the least. The Press men who resemble them most closely are those indefatigable characters in the old 'B' movies with bow-ties, massive cameras supporting lighthouse flash bulbs, hat brims turned up at the front and Press badges stuck in their hat bands. Argentinian journalists delight in turning up at the crack of dawn and rushing in with the waiter bringing breakfast, or sitting on the bonnet of their prey's car until such time as they can get a picture which doesn't require posing the good side and a prearranged 'cheese'. They get interesting photographs that way and are not shy about using them, usually captioning them with something calculated to make a lawyer hesitate about issuing a writ. The paparazzi had a problem with the Grand Prix set. There were so many leggy, suntanned hopefuls running with the pack that it often looked like a herd of buffalo with the bulls flashing gleaming horns for the appreciation of the cows.

The Argentinian Grand Prix used to be the first race of the new season, with the teams trying out newly acquired drivers, hopeful of grabbing a few early points in South America and South Africa which would put them on the European scene, where sponsorship money lay deep and crisp and uneven. But somehow the high endeavour never got under way in the sybaritic atmosphere of the famed 'Paris under the Southern Cross'. There was a carefree, unself-conscious atmosphere unlike that at any of the following venues, when the pace hotted up and the competition became deadly serious.

It was in Buenos Aires that I had a taste of Graham's peculiar sense of humour. Lying on a sunbed by the pool at the Sheraton I happened to mention that it was my birthday. Graham reacted immediately. That very night, he proclaimed, we would have a party. Graham spent the rest of the day putting the word around that there would be a birthday party that evening. The venue was to be at a firm favourite of the Grand Prix set, the *Gatto Negro* in Olivos. It was a fabulous setting, half indoors and half in the open. Outside there were huge semi-globular wickerwork seats hanging from towering sweet-smelling eucalyptus trees, with the light supplied by blazing torches and hundreds of candles. There was a large, irregular-shaped swimming pool with floating tables, and a bar right in the water. It was a great evening. The proprietor did us proud, roping off a comfortable area so that we could develop the party atmosphere and be seen by the customers. Miniskirts were still very much *de rigeur* in the *capital de la noche* and the erotic writhing in time to the music made the night even steamier.

Gradually the guests began to drift away, not a few in extended couples. Graham, well-tanned and relaxed in a Hawaiian-style shirt, white slacks and shoes, primped his moustache with a lascivious leer at a couple of tall leggy blondes who had been doing their best all evening not to have their intentions misinterpreted, and said he was off and would see me in the morning. Saying good night to Graham made me a little uneasy but there was still plenty going on so I dismissed the insecure feeling I was getting and returned to the fun. By the time Mike Hailwood departed, the sun was bleeding into the eastern sky and the club was practically empty. Just as I was shaking hands with the barman prior to wobbling off into the dawn the reckoning came. A beefy forerunner of 'Jaws' Kiel dropped a bill on the bar and looked at me as if he was hoping I wouldn't be able to pay it, which was just about right! Who was paying for my birthday party had not been high on my list of things I wanted to known. I suppose if I had thought of it at all I had expected Graham to sort it out. But he was gone and so were most of the others. Jeff Hutchinson, a prolific journalist who never seems to sleep, managed to come up with a few dollars and this, added to my meagre store, just about covered the tip. Cautiously I had left my money, cheques and credit cards in the the safe at the Hotel. It looked bad. The proprietor, who had been conspicuous all evening by his wide grin and eagerness to pour drinks, appeared to add authority to what 'Jaws' was expected to do to non-paying customers. Just as I was contemplating making a less than hopeful dash for it, my body was saved from having its deformable structure tested by a customer sitting at the far end of the bar! Several times during the evening I had noticed him. He was dark and swarthily handsome with a phosphorescent smile under a wide Don Ameche moustache. Although he hadn't tried to join the party he had obviously enjoyed it. He had a few brief words with the night club owner and scrawled his signature across the bottom of the bill. Reluctantly 'Jaws' was ushered back to the nether regions and I heartily thanked my saviour. His name was Alfredo Dieguez and he was a well-known figure in all sorts of regions of the Argentine economy, especially in trucking and night clubs, where he exercised some control that I was never ungracious enough to question the nature of. He became a good friend, not only to me but to most of the Grand Prix villagers. Next morning I tried to broach the subject of how I had been saved from ending up more compacted than the local corned beef but Graham wasn't very sociable.

The race cars had at last arrived at the circuit and everyone was going to have a look at them to see if they were still raceable after the attentions of the shipping experts and the customs officers, who were unbelievably adept at getting souvenirs. The cars hadn't been expected to see the light of day for at least another couple of days and were considered an intrusion into our idyll. Philosophically, when nobody seemed interested in my tale of woe, I decided to pay up and try to look as if I was enjoying it. Denny Hulme and Mike Hailwood were the only drivers to offer what they considered their proportion of the bill, although Graham did on one occasion half-heartedly ask how much he owed.

Back in the colder, more sobering climate of England there was a lot to do before the March deadline of the South African Grand Prix. Graham liked the fierce, primitive Kyalami race. It held a lot of memories for him and he intended to do well. He also had something else to think about. The Government-sponsored French Matra team had offered him a seat in one of the three official cars they were entering for Le Mans. In recent years Ford, Porsche and Ferrari had tended to grab the headlines and understandably the French were feeling slightly peeved that what was virtually a French monument was being constantly consigned to foreign hands. Graham was privileged to be asked to join the team. It must have been the way he wore his beret. Whatever it was, Graham would be lining up on the grid for the 24-hour bash with the cream of the crop, Parisian elfin Jean Pierre Beltoise, playboy François Cevert, bearded Henri Pescarola and ascetic Jacques Laffite. It meant a punishing work load that kept Graham on the move constantly, first at the Matra Paris headquarters and later at the Paul Ricard circuit for testing. The French were keeping their effort very hush-hush in their determination to produce a winning performance and they didn't want the opposition to get word of what was going on. Graham was impressed with Matra's dedication and Matra was impressed with Graham's ability. The only slight hiccough occurred when Matra decided to have an endurance test to give their drivers confidence that the car would last the course. Graham flew in one mid-morning to be greeted by the Matra team manager with the news that the car had been performing flawlessly for 20 hours. 'I'll soon fix that!' quipped Graham. Half an hour later he was scuttling, red-faced, back aboard the Aztec and setting a course for England. As he said, it was embarrassing. The Matra had put a rod through the side of the block after a couple of laps in Hill's custody. Nevertheless, with Pescarola he won the race.

Left *With tears in his eyes, Graham demonstrates the latest three-point safety belt.*

Below *Graham had time for some quiet grooming while his co-driver, Henri Pescarola, took the Matra over the winning line to take the 1972 Le Mans. For Hill it completed the Triple Crown — Grand Prix Championship, Indianapolis 500 and now Le Mans.*

Graham's ambassadorial qualities were blossoming. He was beginning to represent the up-front salesmen for the sport, and was generally acknowledged to be doing a first class job. He was moving into a new phase of his career, one which he fitted admirably and which he could expand almost limitlessly if he could just control his need to demonstrate his virtuosity behind the steering wheel.

Completely independent of Hill, Alain de Cadinet, a hopeful Le Mans entrant, had been on a converging course with the champion. De Cadinet had for years trodden a fraying tightrope in his efforts to get a car prepared annually for the big race. Usually at the last moment he was able to patch together some sort of deal that would take him across the Channel in June. It entailed a lot of canvassing, promises and crossed fingers and along the way he gleaned information, not necessarily of use to him in the way he hoped but something for the future. On a visit to WD & HO Wills of Bristol he was told that they were flattered that he should think of them but no thanks. At lunch later Alain got the feeling that Wills were not happy with his Le Mans entry on a number of counts. For one thing Le Mans was very much the domain of Gitanes and Gauloise with the ubiquitious Marlboro oozing in wherever a gap needed filling in the publicity facade. Wills' interests in France, and on the Continent in general, were minimal and it would take more money than they were prepared to spend to get Pierre to swap his odiferous Gauloise for a Woodbine. Another unfortunate drawback was that they didn't think the driving talent was likely to attract enough international newsprint to wrap round a small portion of fish and chips.

Alain de Cadinet, well-known in racing circles for his mercurial entrepreneurism, wasn't likely to promote Wills' image enough to justify the extent of the budget Wills would have to supply, even with crack sportscar driver, Chris Craft, thrown in as a mainstay.

'What we would need,' quoted the Wills spokesman, 'Would be someone like Graham Hill. Even then Le Mans wouldn't be sustained enough for us to launch a reasonable sales campaign to make it worthwhile.'

A few days later, at the annual BRDC (British Racing Drivers' Club) beanfeast, fate thrust out a gauntlet. De Cadinet had entered a derelict Formula 1 Brabham for Chris Craft to drive at the end of the 1972 season. Knotted purse strings had made the effort a miserable affair but it had given Alain a tenuous link with Brabham. Talk with Wills had re-energised his saliva glands and the prospect of turning an honest wheel in Formula 1 was very tasty. Knowing how fluid the situation was in the Brabham Motor Racing Development camp, de Cadinet made sure that he got within casual conversation range of Brabham's dictatorial boss, Bernie Ecclestone. Hopefully, he forced into the conversation the idea that Brabham might benefit from his expertise. Used to this sort of approach, Bernie nodded understandingly and pointed across the room to where Graham was holding court to a crush of black tie enthusiasts. There had already been talk about Graham getting together his own team to fit into his new image of the official spokesman for the Grand Prix Association, guarded and guided by the secretary of the CSI, Henry Treu.

Bette Hill at the start of the London to Sidney Marathon.

The Association was to have two main aims. Firstly, to bring all the jealously individual circuit functionaries together to present a united front and ubiquitous standard of competence to the worldwide Grands Prix. Secondly, to present a bright, clean-cut image to a public which was being dazzled by the hurly-burly of the public relations pitch but getting progressively less for its money. It was hoped that Graham Hill's saturnine features and rakish elegance would help the fans overlook the fact that drivers, in general, driving around in ever faster circles, were disappearing into the increasingly enveloping cockpit and full-face helmets. Ostensibly, it was a move to capitalise on the adulation Hill was still getting from the public. Beneath the surface it was designed to get him to take another look at his birth certificate and equate it with his decreasing performance on the track. But the move was too subtle. Graham took it at face value and chomped steadily through a diet of refusals from teams who wanted younger eager lions with 20/20 vision in a Grands Prix cockpit but selective blindness to anything else but the crock of gold beyond the chequered flag.

De Cadinet's timing was just right. Graham always kept an eye on what was moving in other pastures and he was well aware of Alain's ability to make something out of nothing in an effort to get his annual outing to Le Mans. They met a few days later and Hill was even more convinced that De Cadinet could provide the answer he was looking for. He had the nuts and bolts, wheeler-dealer mentality which Graham imagined he shared, although he had never had to try it out in the hard market place of the board room. A loose deal was cobbled together. Alain was to get the active end while Graham pulled in faces and got their interest aroused. There was still the snag of where the car was coming from, but Graham felt that this was only a formality. In the past practically everyone he had met with a view of a corporate bank account had told him that if he ever needed help they were to be his first port of call.

The reality was much bleaker. Suddenly everybody was running for the cover of the board room table and regretting that they had just put all their available cash into this project or that project which they, personally, didn't believe in, but which had received the support of their less astute colleagues. But there was always *next* year! De Cadinet told Hill about the conversation he had had with Wills' PR department. It was enough to put Graham on the line to John Wilson, Chairman of Wills, without delay. They were old acquaintances and the chairman listened patiently enough to call a meeting. Alain and Graham hastily scribbled down some figures that looked about right for running costs and staunchly turned a Nelson-like eye to the nitty-gritty of capital costs for things such as the workshop.

The level on which to sell the package had become obvious. The two most frequent headlines were a variation on the 'Over the Hill' theme, and 'Ambassador to Motor Sport'. Mr Wilson had mentioned this in conversation with Hill and had quipped that if they got their thing together 'the Ambassador would have an Embassy' from which to work. So the selling line was to be high-toned, not involving just another driver demanding money for doing something he wanted to do anyway. Graham Hill was going to bring up the standard and represent the sport as the suave, clean, caring undertaking it was. It even helped that the 'Ambassador' was no reckless young chicken. At 43 years of age he represented the stability and long-term reliability that often seemed to be denied by the annual fatality statistics. Even Graham's non-addiction to tobacco was paraded as a plus. Somehow it seemed to say that it was alright to smoke Embassy because Graham didn't and look how he thrived on it, a piece of Orwellian double-think that defeats argument.

Hill was surprised at the comparative ease with which Embassy switched on. Maybe it was the asking price that kept them interested. They were aware of the telephone numbers applicants were wont to quote when they came with their begging bowl and Hill's estimate of £80,000 looked very reasonable; particularly in view of the exposure and history they were buying. Although they had not been enthused by de Cadinet and his Le Mans aspirations, Graham Hill was a different matter. Especially as he had already that year added the *Vingtquatre Heures du Mans* title to his illustrious bag. Wills could pick up the glory without having the expense of the battle. Details were finalised in February 1973 and there was an instant bonus. Cygnet Films, under Tony Maylam, had got the go-ahead on a Graham Hill film and this was hoped to generate a lot of interest and splash the Embassy name about.

Finding the right car, any car, was more of a problem than had been anticipated. While all the *padrones* were willing to applaud Graham's diplomatic role, they all looked the other way when he started talking about his trackside plans for 1973. Ferrari wouldn't give a non-Italian team the time of day let alone rent out a car. Lotus was tied in with John Players and besides, Graham wasn't about to go back to Chapman after he had been less than staunchly supportive when Hill had wanted a drive after his Watkins Glen accident. March was considered but it still hadn't made that breakthrough into the rarified achievement of Formula 1. McLaren was entrenched in a plethora of public relations excercises with Yardley, a subsidiary of BAT, and Brabham was the team Hill was leaving because it couldn't get it's act togther. Marlboro's affair with the BRM team was getting a little *de trop* and anyway, Big Lou Stanley had his pride. Ken Tyrrell wasn't likely to bend a knee to the embryo team boss however much money he brought with him and Frank Williams was a pit-lane joke.

Graham made the decision to go outside the general run of kit-car builders, where he could rely on getting a hearing when he voiced his opinion on what was what. The UOP (Universal Oil Products) Shadow team had been spending a lot of oil money on getting their cars competitive and Don Nichols, the starry-eyed director in charge, convinced Graham that the coming season of 1973 would be

A relaxed Graham Hill with his Brabham Formula 2 sponsored by the German distillery Jägermeister — 1972.

the one in which they would soar above the dross of the other, more staid teams and prove that you didn't need an over-sexed stallion on your bonnet or to be named after a shoe shop to shine on the billboard. Amid solemn pronouncements of mutual respect a team was conjured into being. For UOP Shadow it was the most exciting thing to happen all year, with the possible exception of the lap-keeper's error which promoted Jackie Oliver to the number one spot for a few moments before he decided that Peter Revson in the Yardley McLaren had taken the Canadian Grand Prix from Emerson Fittipaldi in the JPS, dropping the UOP Shadow to third. Driving the official Shadows were the American George Follmer, basically a Can Am driver drafted into the team to flavour the US connection, and Jackie Oliver, responsible through his commitment in the States for initiating the Formula 1 effort.

Team management wasn't completely new to Graham. In Formula 2 he had run a singleton Brabham for the German Hofmeister Company. The new alliance didn't get to the southern hemisphere Grands Prix but Hill had been hoping that he would tweak up the rather pedestrian Shadow into a fleet-shafted challenger by the time the season started in Europe. The extra three months' preparation didn't seem to benefit the car, the driver or the lumpy relationship between de Cadinet and Hill. Increasingly Graham was being asked when he was going to retire. It had become a major source of irritation and a questioner needed to be armadillo-skinned or pinkly innocent to ask it. The irritation had an element of guilt. Graham knew that he was pushing it. So far he had been lucky. At least he could still walk. A lot of his contempories hadn't been so lucky and their memory and occasionally their widows, haunted the scene. Furthermore, in spite of being completely and selfishly immersed in the scene, the finger-wagging, bourgeois morality was still there colouring his views.

Brought up in an atmosphere that cast the family as a tightly-knit group and the father figure as the template for the growing generation, he often had panicky moments when he felt he was not fulfilling his role. Somewhere, there was locked in him an image of the stern, kindly father who knows what's best for his offspring and wouldn't hesitate to play the 'heavy' when he felt it was called for. He also thought, in deference to the new age, that children should have greater freedom. The conflicting forces made his relationship with his children rather forced and uncertain at times, particularly with Damon. He desperately wanted to be a friend and father to his son but the circumstances were rarely favourable. At the weekends, when there was no school, Graham would be off in some far-flung corner of the world going round and round in circles. In the week, during the day, when occasionally he had an hour or two to spare, Damon was at school. By the time he came home his father would be off entertaining or being entertained until the early hours of the morning. Bette was better able to take it. She had been with Graham since the grey days of factory work and the dole queue. Although, inevitably, he had grown and blossomed with a persona alien to the one she had known earlier, she was able to make the mental adjustment more easily. Damon was proud of his father and desperately wanted to be closer. As it could not be, he tended to become more introspective and independent.

Whatever Graham's intentions were, they were overridden by events. Now he was not only the driver but also the man who must keep the financier's hand hovering above his cheque-book, a role which his abrasive ego fitted not at all. By a superhuman effort, Hill managed to control his exasperation. The Press turn-out helped. As the day for his debut in Spain drew near they moved in. Graham's every move was catalogued and *el viejo* was fêted as fervently as he had ever been.

There is something about the Latin, assuming that that includes the Spanish and South Americans, that makes their condescending hero-worship exciting. Somehow they manage to get across the feeling that they are confirming the subject of their adulation's worth. At times their forceful fanaticism can be too much, especially in Barcelona. The circuit, arguably the most beautiful setting in the world of motor racing, ran through the Montjuich Parque with vistas across the city and harbour. All around the park, delightful little bistros plied stringy steak and rasping red wine to the accompaniment of 400 bhp engines driving through the perilous helter-skleter of Armco-barriered roads. Occasionally a wayward car would add a percussion point by whacking into the barrier to a chorus of *olés* and polite enquiries about the driver's nationality.

It was in this setting that I had really got to know Graham back in 1968. Although we had been on terms of polite chat for a number of years it wasn't until I was team manager for Jack Oliver's Lotus and Jimmy Clark and Graham Hill were piloting the two other Lotus entries, that we became friendly. It was to be Jimmy Clark's last race before the fateful Hockenheim race a week later. For some reason we had taken Jack's Lotus T48 down on a trailer behind a borrowed

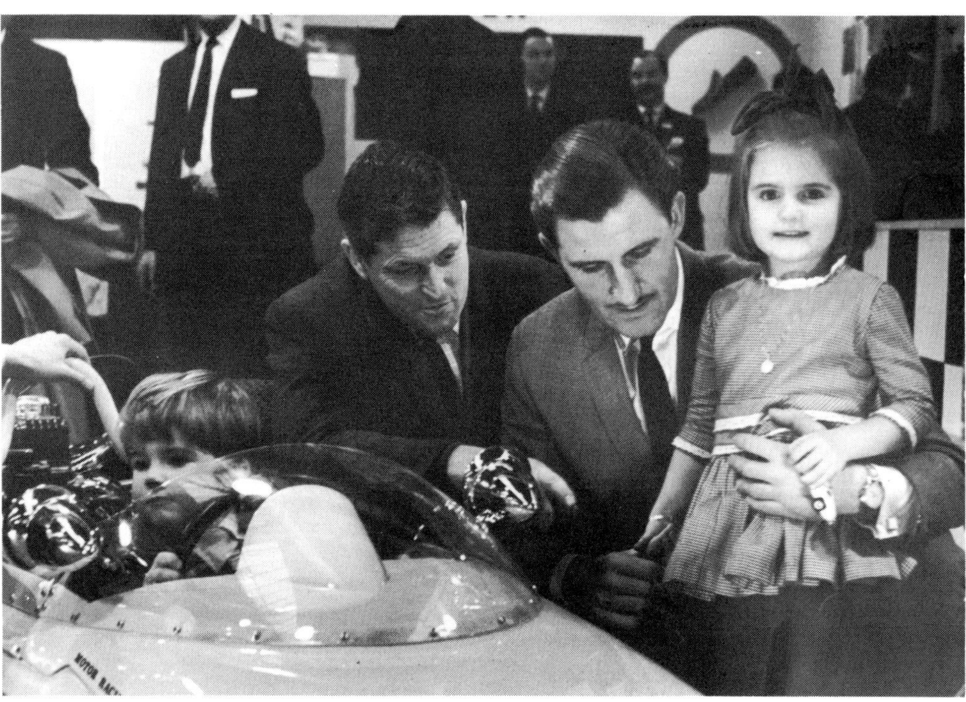

Ford Executive. It meant that we had the only road car and it became the main transportation between the hotel and circuit. The evening before the race, Jimmy, Graham and Jackie had been asked to do their bit at the opening of a Renault Bar. Colin Chapman and I had been asked along as a courtesy. After a few drinks and a lot of boredom, nameplates were fitted behind the drivers' seats by the manager, who declared that any time they came into the bar, no matter who was sitting there, that was where they sat! The vision of trying to unseat a couple of matadors from the bullring across the way was interesting.

As soon as we could, we got away. Jimmy wanted a quiet meal and an early night. Graham fell in line because he had nothing better to offer and the rest of us went along because we weren't consulted. We ended up in the backroom of a side street *bodega* eating *paisano* food that benefitted from the dim light and the noisy atmosphere. Jimmy's desire for a quiet meal took a knock before we had taken the first mouthful. Mindful of the windfall of publicity that had fallen like manna from heaven on his little café, the astute proprietor had rung around the news desks and been blessed with a cohort of flashlighted newshawks trying to get the gastronomic lowdown on the brass of Team Lotus. Jimmy was considerably annoyed but Graham responded in his usual obliging manner and gave the Press what they wanted.

Next morning, through some minor miscalculation, after visiting the track to see that Jack had a car popping on all cylinders, I went back to the hotel to pick up the heavyweights. It was a bit of a crush. Jimmy insisted on driving and I sat in the front with Graham on my lap. In the back there was even more of a crush.

Left *At the Racing Car Show, Damon gets some time behind the wheel, while Graham plays Dad to Brigitte.*

Right *A useful form of transport on the roads and in the paddock on race day.*

From somewhere Jimmy had conjured up a couple of female fans and Chapman had invited along a Spaniard he had met in the bar the previous evening and hadn't had the opportunity to give the slip to. One of the girls was sitting on the other's lap, and Colin was jammed in the middle of the seat between them and his sweaty Spanish friend, while Jack was crouching on the floor and leaning on the consul between the two front seats. Luckily the distance from hotel to paddock was only about 2 miles. Unfortunately, at that time, everyone who possessed wheels within 500 miles of Barcelona was funnelling through the same narrow streets. As the minutes ticked away I began to get nervous. Although I had been on time to pick them up I could see the ordure dripping slowly past my ears if we didn't make the circuit in time. I tried to propitiate the gods by pointing out that we hadn't moved for about five minutes and at that rate we were going to be lucky if we got to the pits before they ran out the chequered flag. Jimmy smiled sympathetically but said nothing. Graham wasn't so reticent. 'They won't start without us!' he explained. 'We are the race!'

Jimmy's race was soon run. On the opening lap he was pushed off by Jacky Ickx. He wasn't happy. Graham wasn't exactly bubbling brown sugar either. He had started half way back on the grid and maintained that position until his engine ingested a valve half way through the race. Colin Chapman was anxious to get away. He had flown down in his plane and wanted to get clear of the airport before nightfall. The Continentals have a thing about private planes floating around after dark. He grabbed the keys of the Ford and disappeared. I found the car a couple of hours later standing on the side of the runway, doors gaping open, where he had left it. And have you ever tried to get a car, which shouldn't have been there in the first place, out of a Spanish airport? They say adversity strengthens the soul. Getting cars out of Spanish airports should be part of the qualification for a Duke of Edinburgh Award. Jack and I got back to the hotel just in time to have dinner with Jimmy and French journalist Jabby Crombac. A week later, while I was at Brands Hatch for the BOAC 500 with Jack in the Lotus Europa, the news came through that Jimmy had been killed at Hockenheim.

In the years since that traumatic announcement little had changed at Montjuich in 1973 except the Marlboro signs which now seemed to dominate everything.

Chapter 5

Groupies' delight

Camp followers have always been an important part of any army. When the Roman legions were stomping in manly cameraderie in arrow-straight lines across Europe, there was a multi-national wake of ladies of varied virtue following. Just what the attraction was is hard to understand now. It certainly wasn't the food. The Roman soldier was the forerunner of the Scot when it came to porridge. It was much later that the quaint idea that an army marches on it's stomach was mooted. In recent wars the camp followers have been dressed up in a uniform, given a rank and taught how and who to salute. A practice that didn't exist in less formal times.

But wars, they tell us, are a barbarism of the past. Now there are minor skirmishes but they don't count. This could have been disastrous for the trade of camp-follower if a minor social revolution hadn't rendered entertainment a major endeavour in the second half of the 20th century. It wasn't that there was any new danger attached to entertainment, it was just that violence which had formerly been subjugated to state causes now found an outlet in music and sport. This doesn't necessarily mean that sport has become more brutalised. On the contrary, contests to the death are frowned on. The nearest thing to gladiatorial combat which still survives is boxing.

The army then, having lost it's glamour along with it's red jackets and razor edged sabres, left the camp followers feeling cheated. The excitement they needed was to be found with the pop groups and the sportsmen. All sports attract a following, but motor racing is unique in the quality of the female camp followers it attracts. The age range varies from the gymslip privateers up to groovy grannies who come on strong and hard in an attempt to get the thrill of a last climactic encounter. Between the extremes is the hard core of sexy, well-dressed ladies who describe themselves variously as models, public relations managers, actresses, time-keepers or just plain 'friends of'. It is easy to dismiss them as brainless hangers-on whose main interest is to complete a gridful of names who they can claim they have dropped their knickers to. A lot of them do seem to have this as their main motivation. Nevertheless, their presence on the scene is almost as essential as the mechanics' and often more important than the team manager. A driver hasn't arrived until he can boast a full complement of 'ponies', 'corralled' at the track side as a status symbol. They are there to gratify him when he does well or take his anger when he can't get it together.

There are two main types. Type one is the pure-bred groupie. When hot pants were the rage hers were so brief they frequently disappeared up her buttock cleavage. She always sports a suntan, usually accompanied by startling blue eyes and long, fine blonde hair. She's everybody's friend. She usually has a thick streak of nymphomania, and is the one you hear the stories about. She vies with the others to be the first to have had everyone on the grid. These are the ones who strip off at the parties and dance on the table or drive from one circuit to the next with three or four blokes who are serviced more regularly than Roger Clarks' Rally car. They usually survive about two seasons then wander off to wherever groupies go when they have outgrown their groupieness at one venue.

The second type is more classy. They usual run to tailored jeans, Lanvin shirts and Gucci shoes. They are equally active but in a more refined manner. They have a withdrawn air, appearing to be perched on a tyre on the pit counter as a favour to the organiser. They tend to be less fun than the groupie Mark One but they are deadlier. They aren't there for the thrill of another helmet to hang on their Gucci belt. They are there for what they can get out of it. That doesn't mean pounds, Deutsche Marks or whatever, since they usually have enough of the folding stuff to pay their own way. What they are looking for is self-aggrandisement, not always with the commercial aspect in mind. It just gives them a thrill to hit the gossip columns occasionally, to have a picture of themselves sitting in their St Honoré splendour on a yacht at Monte Carlo or skiing at Gstaad, with a recently rich and famous racing driver.

More honest about their motivation are the models and starlets who use the drivers to break through the barriers into the land where the honey pot is always full and a glamourous weekend can earn the promise of a hand up with a flagging career. However often they are disappointed, they keep making the running, sure that next time their casting couch philosophy will work.

Separated by a thick true-blue line, and often a gold band, are the regular girl friends and wives. These parade around the paddock secure in the knowledge that they have got what every girl wants, though at close quarters it is often not what was promised. Over the years the sacred cow syndrome has developed around these ladies and they are treated with respect by everyone, even the good-time, well-cleavaged bandits. The 'Legits' have even banded together to form an exclusive club which they have named 'The Doghouse Owners' Club'. Even that's not what it used to be. In the late '60s and early '70s the names in the club were reflected on the grid. Bette Hill was, and still is, the leading light and driving force. Around her she gathered the spouses of the notables; Sally Courage, Nina Rindt, Patty McLaren, Marianne Bonnier, Nelly Pace, Mimicha Reutemann, Marie-Helena and Susie Fittipaldi, Janet Brise, June Birrell, Debbie Rees, Barbro Peterson and Lynne Oliver. There were also a few 'companions' who were let in. Ostensibly the aim of the club was to be a focal point for wives separated from their husbands because of their duties at the track—either as drivers or in a lay capacity. Few non-drivers' wives seemed to penetrate the enclave. A notable exception is Eba Grant, wife of the late Gregor Grant who founded *Autosport*. As the motor racing scene has become less of a community

Doghouse Owners' Club at Silverstone just before the start of the 1969 British Grand Prix. Left, Sally Courage and Nina Rindt, background, Bette Hill and Antoinette Lucas.

and more of a horse trading circle the Doghouse Owners' Club has dwindled away. Now it is only the fierce efforts of Bette and Eba which keep it going. Anyway, basically this line-up exists now, existed when Graham was gracing the scene and will probably go on for some time to come.

What galavanised it in the '60s and '70s was the new sense of liberation which was sweeping aside old and tried concepts and replacing them with a wild disorder which was dubbed 'permissiveness'. No more was a flash of stocking looked on as something shocking, now everything was paraded. Mary Quant even tried to redirect attention from the orgy of bra burning by focusing on the pubic hair. Sex was fun and no longer something confined to the bedroom or the back of the family saloon. At least that was what the gurus said, turning a blind eye to the misery and pain of abortion and the increase in sexually transmitted diseases. Nowhere were there to be found more sexually uninhibited dolly birds than surrounding the pop scene and the race track.

For someone like Graham Hill, with his middle class morality, his enhanced value as a sex symbol had a big impact. He was expected to react in a lascivious manner whenever a female walked by, whether she was nine or ninety made no difference. Everybody agreed that Graham Hill had it made and that he had more 'crumpet' than Carter had peanuts. He enjoyed his reputation and tried to live up to it as much as possible. The scene seemed to have been waiting for him. As he donned the laurels of a victor, the last lace of Victorian prudery was snipped away. The heroes were now a shambling, inarticulate Neanderthal, known as Elvis 'the Pelvis', and those such as Christine Keeler and Mandy Rice Davies,

the twins of the sinning metropolis. The temptation to stray had always been there. Men have a worse time resisting temptation than women. If a woman declines an invitation it's considered proper. A man who does the same thing is a creature of scorn and ridicule. While men were doing the chasing and women were doing the refusing all was right with the world.

Suddenly all that changed. An incautious request for a dance could lead to a medical examination in a dreary green-painted shack discretely hidden from the eyes of the hospital proper. For Graham and the other men touched by the glamour of death there was a nervous provocative mass of pulchritude on offer at every turn. The easy accessibility and the boundless supply produced a reaction in the drivers that was not complimentary to women as a whole. Innuendo took the place of casual conversation. The drivers felt they were living in a Sultan's paradise where anyone in a miniskirt was a personal hand-maiden. What they didn't realise was that they were the hunted. Graham never seemed to sort out what was going on. Indiscriminately he chatted up every woman who crossed his path. Few objected and those who did were dismissed as being spoilsports.

The fear which dominated Graham and made him the soul of discretion was the fear that Bette might find out. He knew he was surrounded by plenty of would-be informers only too ready to drop the word. He was like a dog which has just eaten the sausage on the table and is waiting for its master to find out. Cheered on by his reputation and the need to be admired, Graham flung himself into the life of a rake with wilful abandonment, but constantly nagged by his conscience. The older he got the more contemptuous of women he became. His chatting-up became an insolent proposition which he neither cared about nor was willing to spend time on. Basically Graham was a coward in his relationships with women. He wanted to fulfill his reputation but he didn't want the traumas of actual commitment. In Salzburg he was attacked in his bedroom by a young girl who turned out to be only fifteen. Aghast Graham made sure that he had someone present all the time so that he wouldn't find himself standing in the dock. It would have been easier to tell the girl firmly to go back to school, but she was young and hero-worshipping and it gratified his ego to have her around. He wasn't so happy about it when she turned up in London a few months later, looking for him! He became a moving target and several friends were lined up to make sure that she didn't make any contacts which might have proved embarrassing. In the end he paid for her to return to Salzburg. It was a constant dread that she might make claims that would attract publicity.

It wasn't only the young girls who gave him problems. In Rheims he attended a party given by Freddy Chandon of the famous Champagne family. In the smart international jet set Graham was on top of his form. It was before his view of women had become soured and he was laying on the compliments with a trowel. There was one tall, sophisticated woman, obviously French, who managed to stick with him all evening. Gracious and refined, dressed in the little black silk evening dress which marked her as a woman of breeding, she was as far removed from the accepted idea of a groupie as you could get. After the party we all

Left *Marlboro went for long-legged, blond-haired charmers in hot pants in their effort to sell their motor racing connection to the public.*

Right *Keeping his cool to prove he's been kissed before.*

gathered at the famous Bridgette's bar in Rheims. Graham wasn't there, which was unusual. Later, just around the corner, I spotted him sitting in the corner of a neon-lit restaurant. Next to him, still as elegantly poised as ever, was the Parisienne in the little black number. I smiled and nodded knowingly. Frantically Graham beckoned me in. He had run out of small talk and was sufficiently in awe of the poised woman at his side to not know what to do. We sat and chatted about nothing while the lady smoked her way through a packet of Kent, until, bored, I got up to leave. To try to delay my going Graham tried to get me interested in the wine glasses the restaurant was using. A plastic stem on a glass bowl. For that we were sitting up half the night in the glamorous Champagne country? It was just an example of Graham getting hoisted on his own petard. There was always a streak of uncertainty, an adolescent naivity in him that could be touched off by anyone ready to see through the facade of assertion and aggression and keep coming back. It confused Graham. He expected those around him to show the right amount of respect and pliability. When faced with a flat-eyed matron with larceny on her mind he was reduced to a lonely teenager with nowhere to hide. As long as he was initiating the play he was a brilliant centre forward.

Another instance of rapid back pedalling in a situation not planned by Hill came about in Rhodesia. He was there for a bunfight connected with one of the motoring clubs in Salisbury. They wanted to do a Grand Prix and Hill was the

man doing the talking. I was going somewhere else but somehow I found myself in Salisbury. It was to be a lightning visit. Graham was off next day for another crack at Beirut. Breathless, we rushed around looking at patches of scrubland and tried to orientate them with imaginative drawings of what the artist thought the area would look like embellished with four miles of tarmac and a skyfull of concrete stands.

In the evening we dined at someone's house, either the president of the car club or the visionary architect, before pleading an early morning flight and disappearing. Next to our hotel there was a small plush bar, all soft lights and crushed velvet. Graham wasn't feeling tired so we dropped in there and he fenced with the barman until he got a hot drink of cocoa or something. We found comfortable seats in the corner and sucked at the thick, acrid brew wishing we hadn't bothered. We were just about to go when a good-looking bloke in a white suit slipped into the seat opposite and went into the routine about how he was Graham's number one fan. He seemed to know all about Graham's reasons for being in Salisbury and dropped names like a railway announcer. Something he said seemed to spark Graham off, and in a couple of minutes they were chatting away like a couple of old ladies at a tea party. Before I knew what was happening we were in the back of a car heading for the rich side of the city. We swept through the gates of a bush-lined drive and pulled up outside a bungalow the size of a football stadium. There was no holding back, within minutes we were in an Olympic-sized swimming pool, being handed drinks from white-gloved beings who, in the half-light, looked like stand-ins for the invisible man. Without announcement half a dozen giggling girls appeared and plunged into the pool. Round-eyed, I waited for them to attack me, but deflated when they made a bee-line for Graham. For about ten minutes he stood in amongst them, hands darting maniacally with the flurried precision of an inquisitive octopus, before Graham heaved himself out of the pool and disappeared into the little kraal-type dressing room. I hoped my luck had changed. Since the main attraction had sidelined for the moment, the nubile, sunburned bodies were willing to dally with the understudy. All thoughts of a more starring role disappeared when Graham came out of his hut dressed, and ready to seek out his puritan bed. I don't known who was the most startled, me or the girls. Our new-found friend got quite nasty. It seemed that he had been hoping to lay on a group encounter. Graham told me to stay and enjoy myself but I could tell he didn't mean it. Our newly qualified ex-friend wouldn't even give us a ride back to town, so we had to get a taxi. In the taxi I complained about getting my supply cut off. He wasn't very sympathetic. At first he said that the reason he had opted out was that he thought it was a set-up. There were hidden photographers and cameramen hiding in the bushes eager to get his exploits on emulsion. Later he said that he didn't like being taken for a ride. The bloke had asked him back for a drink. He had no right to invite all his lady friends in for a cheap thrill. To me it looked like a generous act of kindness but then my lifestyle is usually about as exciting as the hole in Orphan Annie's left sock.

There were times when Graham's wildly roaming eye got him into trouble. At a club-cum-disco hidden away somewhere in the Black Forest he narrowly escaped being cut down to size by some of the local foresters. A lot of the Formula 2 drivers had heard about the place in the forest and along with mechanics and journalists turned out to savour the night life. It was more of a restaurant than a club and everyone was forced to eat great platefuls of goulash, swilled down with huge steins of beer. It was that kind of place. You paid your money and they slapped the fare in front of you—take it or leave it. Later the lights were turned down and an enthusiastic Bavarian band had a stab at a few rock and roll numbers. The party began to pick up. Girls from God knows where drifted in and draped themselves around the walls. In spite of the spectrolights and quadrophonic sound it was all very much Saturday night at the village hall. Mike Hailwood, never one to accept depression before the small hours, did his languid imitation of Richard Harris trying to look like Mike Hailwood and started a few maidenly hearts twittering. Graham, not to be outdone, slid like a well-greased serpent into a vacant seat beside a well endowed Saxon lady and ran through his repertoire of leers. He was still leering when the floor was cleared of the half dozen or so couples trying to fit frenetic disco dancing to the oom-pah-pah music. With carefully rehearsed yells of spontaneous happiness a group of men ran in wearing *Lederhosen* with braces and cute little Tyrolean hats with feathers. Without more ado they launched into a phantasmagorical presentation of what wood choppers do. Laughter was not supposed to be the reaction, and it upset the assembled foresters! Of course, the *Fräulein* in the dirndl who Graham was moving in on happened to be the *Mädchen* of the biggest and hairiest knee slapper in the business. Suddenly, everyone was scuffling and trying to get out of the door at the same time. What actually happened isn't too clear. Graham was urging the dancers on to greater excesses when the head axe man dived across to the bar and grabbed him. Instantly everyone jumped forward or backward as was their wont. I found myself legging through the night with Mike Hailwood and a few of the mechanics. Graham wasn't at all amused at the desertion but it later transpired that he had, in fact, got out before us and been given a lift back to the hotel by one of his mechanics.

Chapter 6

Scene from the back

Practice at Barcelona in 1973 had been bloody awful. Whatever Hill and his frantic mechanics tried, the Embassy Shadow displayed all the dynamism of a decrepit milk float. But it didn't matter how much the Hill jaw jutted, on the track the best he could nail down was a supporting role on the last row of the grid. It was obvious that there was a clash of personalities. Alain de Cadinet, still smarting from his reduced circumstances, felt he was being unfairly picked on and reacted with petulance and visible disdain. Graham was being very positive and quoting his homilies about getting the job done, and there not being such a thing as luck, and 'can't' not being in the dictionary. It didn't move the Shadow's position from the rear end of the grid one iota.

Once the race started, the earlier depression dissolved into utter misery. With the brakes a cherry red, Graham was finding stopping fraught with doubt. Coming into the pits, which he did frequently, didn't help put the problem right but it gave driver and team manager a chance to compare smoking eyeball with bristling moustache. To add to the pain, George Follmer, in the quicker of the UOP Shadows, moved up to finish in third spot. It was the famed race of attrition beloved of headline writers, and Graham felt that he had been well and truly worn away. A flurry of hands and thrusting faces was evident around and in the Shadow trailer after the race. Don Nichols was not having any lip from Graham. Proudly he pointed to George Follmer, not the handiest of drivers, and his third place in a similar car, and he in only his second Grand Prix! To point out that ten cars had dropped out in front of him including Jack Oliver in the sister Shadow, to promote him to third place, would have been churlish and unsportsman-like, but understandable. Overheated Hill could not resist the temptation and pointed out that if half the field hadn't disintegrated in front of him the American whizz-kid would have been thirteenth. If Hill could have seen that for the remainder of the year a Shadow wasn't going to figure higher on the starting grid than half way, and that in most races a Shadow (frequently driven by Hill) was going to be on the back row, he would probably have hung up his helmet there and then. As it was he still thought he could forge the Shadow into something less nail-like than it obviously was.

Like John Surtees and Dan Gurney, Graham had always been a tinkerer, driving many a level-headed mechanic to an epithet unusual in the cloister-like environs of the pit lane. Now his tinkering became obsessional. By the time the teams moved to the Mickey Mouse circuit on the edge of the little Flemish town of Zolder, many a bright eye had glistened a tear and many a throat had been cleared. The fact that the race was being held there in deference to politics didn't help matters. The GPDA, the elite drivers' trades union, had given Spa, the time-honoured venue for the Belgian Grand Prix, the thumbs down, and the Belgian authorities had hastily laid out a featureless circuit, suitable for the safety-conscious, just outside Brussels at Nivelles. Unfortunately that upset the Belgians on the Flemish side so it was decided to take a leaf out of the British programme and alternate the Grands Prix between two circuits; one year in Nivelles and the next at Zolder. The most ambitious race that had been held there

Graham discusses the Embassy Formula 1 Shadow at the new Feltham Factory. Later discussions were to be less placid, 1973.

The 'Ambassador to Motor Sport' displays his Embassy, 1973.

before was Formula 2, so it meant spending a lot of money to bring the track up to anything like Grands Prix drivers' specifications.

Right up until the start of practice at Zolder the more vociferous members of the GPDA, by definition Jackie Stewart and Niki Lauda, were trying to get it cancelled. Hardy little groups of drivers could be seen walking the course, measuring Armco barriers and kicking at the tarmac with their heels in an effort to break up the newly laid surface. Poor Peter Westbury, the official examiner of tracks for the GPDA, shuffled around on the fringes, embarrassed by the scorn with which the drivers were treating the amenities of the circuit which he had pronounced fit for work. It wasn't a happy time for any of the teams and in the Embassy camp, exchanges were anything but diplomatic. When Graham wasn't out heeling the track, he was in the garage toeing the mechanics. What was needed was a strong team manager to take the hassle and keep the heat away from the mechanics. Used to having his own way with his own equipe, de Cadinet was not in the mood to take the Hill invective quietly. By the time of the final day's practice, when Graham found himself again on the back row of the grid with Jack Oliver in a similar car one row up and one and a half seconds faster, something had to give, and at dinner that night it gave.

The Embassy equipe was staying at a little hotel favoured by drivers, called Boudenberg. There's a big, open log fire with comfortable armchairs around it and the dining room leads off into a rustic, wooden-beamed, split-level bulge. Graham had sorted out a table in an out of the way corner. He was sick and tired of the slightly patronising way people had of asking him what was wrong with the car, as if they knew that it was really the nut behind the wheel that needed tightening. Peter Dyke, the Embassy PR man, and Bette affected not to notice the build-up of static in the atmosphere as they chatted inconsequentially together. Graham pushed through his first course without a word while Alain tried to pretend he wasn't there. Hill carefully wiped his mouth and looked across at de Cadinet.

'Have the mechanics had their dinner yet?' he asked innocently. Alain shook his head in a disinterested way. 'Well, why the fuck not?' Graham demanded, all pretence at lack of interest gone. 'You're supposed to be the bloody team manager, before you sit down on your fat arse you should see that they are all right. Christ knows what time they are going to finish poncing about on that bloody nail of a car and I don't want them knocking off before it's finished!' He paused and de Cadinet tried to get in a word in his defence but Hill had worked up a good head of steam now and was gripping the rails. 'What are you doing here anyway? Your job is to stay in the pits to see that the car is ready for the morning. When you're sure that there is nothing else to do, that's when you leave the garage and not before!' Hill spelled out the working conditions. De Cadinet looked for a moment as if he was going to get into the show but decided against it. He stood up. 'Where are you going?' Graham demanded, although he knew the answer. 'To the garage.' Alain said unctuously. 'Sit down.' Hill shouted. 'I have to do everything else myself, I might as well do this.' Alain watched Graham's self-righteous back disappear through the door and then left the restaurant.

Isola 2000, a ski resort about 50 miles north of Nice, opened to big press coverage in 1974. Graham was there with his family to help out.

Next morning the weather was ideal for a big turn-out. Not too hot, but sunny, with a break in the weather not forecast until late in the day. Around the Embassy pit the atmosphere was arctic. Dyke was prudently keeping out of the way, distributing handouts to anyone who would take one. Bette, an old campaigner, kept out of Graham's way and affected not to detect the frost. The time for the race approached with the argument as to whether to race or not being bandied about in the GPDA trailer in spite of the thousands of people filing into the stands.

Ronnie Peterson was the immediate cause of the discussion over circuit suitability. The Swede had qualified his JPS Lotus well, 0.14 of a second in front of Denny Hulme in the Yardley McLaren. Then, in the untimed practice half hour, which had recently become an accepted part of the routine of race mornings, he had taken out two cars and promptly stuffed them into the catch fencing. The problem had been due to the tarmac breaking up on some of the tighter corners and providing 'marbles' of rubber in awkward places. Minor surgery to the track was carried out by the race officials and reluctantly Stewart agreed that the race could go ahead.

Graham went back to the pit garage and stood, head sunk on his chest, with an aura that spoke louder than any neon sign that he was not to be disturbed. Somehow a spectator, innocence his protection, ducked under the string barrier and, trailing two small children, approached the statue-like Hill. He was the only one who didn't see what was happening and everyone froze, waiting for the strident reaction which seemed inevitable. The fan, with a happy smile on his face, tugged at Graham's arm. He didn't move for what seemed like an hour, then his face flushed and he swung round ready to spew up some of the pent up bile that had built up over the last couple of days. Before he could get going, the unsuspecting fan thrust his two pretty six-year-old daughters forward and waved a strictly snapshot, plastic camera in front of him with the assurance of a flash David Bailey. 'Please, Mr. Hill!' he pleaded. 'I take your photograph with my little girls.' Blind luck had made him press the right button. One thing Graham wasn't about to do, guilt-complex and all, was make himself an ogre in front of a couple of kids, or make their adoring dad look foolish. The mechanics looked on unbelievingly as the flustered fan tried to get his act together with the camera and Graham hunched down between the little girls, chatting and tickling them until the father had clicked off a few memorable shots. He then went back to his morose contemplation of his non-performing race-ware. As it turned out the efforts of the mechanics had not been entirely in vain. Graham didn't pick up any points but he finished (which was more than either of the official Shadows did), in ninth place.

One of Graham's outstanding qualities was his loyalty to those he considered to be sharing his umbrella. It wasn't necessarily a long-term affair but while it lasted he could be relied upon. Equally, when it was all over, it was quite plain that even the time of day was too much to expect. Going to Hockenheim for a Formula 2 meeting I flew down with Graham in the Aztec. By now, although I was qualified, I had learned not to offer advice or pass remarks on Graham's flying.

Not that there was anything derogatory to say. He was a careful, systematic pilot who concentrated totally on what he was doing. There is a saying amongst the flying fraternity, 'There are old pilots and bold pilots but no old, bold pilots!' Graham definitely came into the old pilot category. Flying with him all over the Continent over a period of four years there was never once an occasion when he was not fully in control and competent to deal with the situation. At Hockenheim we were met by Graham's German sponsors. As usual there was most of the PR department and Press milling around and he was hustled off to the waiting cars. It all happened so quickly I could only stand and watch. Suddenly Graham squeezed back out of the car and waved to me. There was no more room in his car so he got hold of the PR man and waited while they sorted out how I was going to get to the hotel. He was always like that. Not a quality found in many of the other top racing drivers, who are prepared, at the drop of a sponsor's decal, to leave anyone they are with to sort out their own salvation while they feed noisily at the trough. That same evening Graham insisted that a space be made for me at a dinner given in his honour by the local motoring club. He was in great form. The more staid members of the club began to drift off about midnight but Graham had only just got into his stride. With a few of the stalwarts still hanging around he ran through his huge repertoire of songs learned in the Navy and the rowing club. They got progressively bluer as the night wore on, but it didn't matter. The audience was now down to Grahame White, shiny and pink, looking like Billy Bunter at the Harrods hamper and well able to join in the chorus, a German lady photographer who was hoping for more than a flash, and me, capable of underscoring the basic, repetitive motif of the cadenzas. The remaining Germans, excellent in their Berlitz way, found the general trend of the words familiar but beyond them, although latterly they began to pick up the basic four letter words and belt them out more or less accurately.

Graham's ability to keep going was legendary. There seemed never to be a moment when he just wanted to sit back and relax. The nearest he ever seemed to come to this state was immediately before a race. This was only window dressing. Beneath the calm exterior and the air of bored languor his brain seethed with speculations, calculations, hopes and quite a healthy dollop of good old-fashioned fear. The frequently published pictures of Graham sitting on a pit counter yawning his head off had nothing to do with boredom or fatigue. It had a lot to do with fear releasing an above-average amount of adrenalin and the need for his pounding heart to take aboard added oxygen.

An example of Graham's prodigious energy came the morning after carousing to the wee small hours. A car had been laid on by his sponsor, Jägermeister, to take us all to the track early in the morning. At seven Graham smashed open my bedroom door and told me that if I wasn't ready in five minutes I would have to make other arrangements for getting to the circuit. Once he was safely out of the way I buried my head under the pillow and prayed he wouldn't return. He didn't and later I managed to cadge a lift to the track. I spent a lot of the morning sprawled in one of the Goodyear hospitality huts trying to convince myself that my state was reversible, but not having much success. The only time I caught

Knees up Mother Brown! An impromptu cabaret at the Monaco Sporting Club dinner held in the Hotel de Paris. Star attractions were Graham, François Cevert and Jackie Stewart.

sight of Graham he was striding purposefully across the paddock with a journalist from some magazine who was interested in putting him through some sort of driving test. I preferred not to know. Later, when I was feeling less delicate, I found him arranging to go off to an American Air Force base with Peter Gethin and Grahame White to play golf. I moved myself in, hoping that a brisk walk and some vicious swiping might do me some good. The reason we had chosen a US base was that Germany isn't the most golf conscious nation in the world and Germans prefer to use their land resources for building economically useful steel works or for cultivating heavy cropping fodder, rather than for non-utilitarian golf courses. The Americans have different priorities.

So there we were in the middle of the afternoon, borrowing clubs and shoes from the ever-generous GIs and setting out to demolish their course. After the usual arguments about the number of strokes who was giving whom, and what it was going to cost the loser, Graham suggested a novel variation. His sponsors had given him a crate of their brew which he just happened to have in the boot of the borrowed car. I'm sure that there's a German of impeccable taste who will tell you that Jägermeister products are ace. Let's charitably say that they are an acquired taste and compare it unfavourably with friar's balsam. The twist Graham was introducing to golf was this: the winner of the hole took two measures of the brew and the loser one. The idea was that the winner would more

quickly lose his edge and the loser would become more relaxed. The system worked. As the afternoon slipped by and fortunes changed everybody got quite a taste for the thick black liquid. Its effect on our golf wasn't noticeably beneficial. The state of play by the time the light began to fade was a little erratic. We were still two holes from home when the light failed completely. By this time we didn't care. As we blundered our way up the eighteenth, laughing hysterically and using lighters and matches in a futile attempt to find our balls, we were joined by some of the Americans from the club. At last they managed to convince us that we weren't going to find the balls and we joined them at the bar. After that the evening recollections become somewhat hazy. I think I probably caught some sort of a virus complaint or maybe the drinks were drugged. All I know was it was well into the next day before I was able to surface. When I finally got to the circuit, Graham was pounding around pretending nothing had happened. I was happy to see that even he was looking a bit waxen about the eyes but to anyone not in the know he looked his normal manic self.

The prolonged merry-making was probably just a way for Graham to push away the gloom and the thought that now he really was out on his own. Not only in Formula 2, which he always considered the lighter side of his commitment, but also in the deadly serious world of Grands Prix. After the Monaco Grand Prix that year he was to be even more on his own. The situation between team manager Alain de Cadinet and driver-cum-patron had deteriorated to such an extent that the few words they were forced to exchange were as easily transmitted as Hail Marys in a synagogue. Whatever the situation off the track, on it the team manager has to be The Man.

Graham, at the beginning of their relationship, had given all control to de Cadinet. It was the sort of open-handed gesture common in new undertakings. It is as commonly regretted at a later date. How long it survives is dependent on the pressure. The pressures on the Hill/Embassy/de Cadinet alliance were pretty cataclysmic. Predictably the money from Wills, based on the Hill/de Cadinet estimate, hadn't been enough. To run the team it might have been adequate but to start it from scratch it was not much more than a hire-purchase deposit. A veteran of this situation, de Cadinet manoeuvred and schemed, getting a favour here and a helping hand there, keeping the boat afloat and praying for someone to raise a breeze. Graham, a cossetted works driver from the start of his driving career, knew nothing about this side of the business. He just knew he wasn't getting results and he blamed it on his team manager. Peter Dyke, the fly on the wall for Embassy, was aware of the conflict. New to motor sport, he was not in a good position to know what to do about it. On the surface it looked as if his fate was tied in with Hill so he let him know that Embassy would not be too unhappy if there was a change of team manager. It was too much for Graham. With all his problems, both personal and professional, he wasn't going to go out on a limb for someone he felt wasn't pulling his weight.

The garage for the race cars at Monte Carlo is underground just off the

Left *The tension mounts. Waiting to take his place on the grid for the start of a race.*

Now look 'ere you. . . the idea is . . . to hit the ball. . . and. . . sod it!

Princess Grace Boulevard along the coast. From there to the pit area is about a mile. In the old days it was quite natural for team managers or mechanics to drive the car down for the driver. Lately it is more usual for the cars to be delivered on a trailer. In 1973 it was a 50/50 situation. Unfortunately de Cadinet chose the wrong 50 and decided to drive Graham's Shadow to the pits. Hill was outraged. Instead of apologising and backing off, de Cadinet told him that he had enough experience of DFV engines and motor racing in general to be able to undertake a simple drive through the streets without doing any harm. It was the wrong attitude to take. Savagely Graham wiped his team manager out of the picture. All through practice he spoke directly to the mechanics ignoring any help offered by de Cadinet.

Monaco was crucial for the Hill ego. Five times he had mastered the tricky, round-the-houses circuit and on other occasions chalked up seconds and a third. With his own team, and a responsibility to his backer, he drove himself to the borders of hysteria trying to put a competitive car together. Most of the time he seemed to be going backwards. His desperation drove him to wild adjustments,

which, under a strong team manager in an established team, would have been sidetracked. For Bette it was a horrible day. Staunchly supporting Graham she innocently wandered into the firing line to receive a volley of abuse which had the mechanics cringing and wishing they could be somewhere else, and all this under the eye of the film crew and the Press wanting to know if this, his 150th Grand Prix appearance, was going to be his swan song. His race was little short of disastrous and painful to all the spectators who remembered the Monarch of Monaco in the days of his glory. Frequent pit-stops did nothing to elevate his position from the back of the field and there was a universal sigh of relief when he dropped out with a reported suspension failure, at the three quarter mark. It caused Tony Maylam, who was making a film about Graham, and his crew even more problems. Not only had they caught the cavalier being less than courteous but they also had the spectacle of him trailing around at the back of the field. Their hopes of filming Hill yet again bending a knee to Rainier and Grace seemed doomed until the Prince agreed to put on a special appearance for Graham. After all, it was Graham's dexterity at negotiating the Principality's streets that had helped to keep him in business, but it was the end of the short-lived Hill/de Cadinet alliance.

Back in England Graham called him into his office and told him that their mutual future ended there. In a way it was a relief to de Cadinet, who felt near to mental collapse. It gave him the time he needed to attend to his own Le Mans entry and forget about pushing into Grands Prix racing for a while. The decision also helped to steady Graham. It made him take a step back and see just what was happening to him. Consciously he forced himself to relax, to try to take a more rational view of his position. The Shadow was a dead duck, confirmed by the performance of the two works cars. The fact that the car had been put together by John Thompson specifically for Graham outside the Shadow factory workshop meant nothing to the sponsor. He had been promised a winning combination. Graham had to keep everything sweet and plan for better things next year.

A few weeks later we flew up to Anderstorp for the newly inaugurated Swedish Grand Prix. It had been organised by a local character masquerading under the name of Smoky Ansberg who had seized the opportunity of bringing big time racing to Sweden in the wake left by the Scandinavian aces Ronnie Peterson and Reine Wisell. Formula 2 racing had been just about surviving at Kinekulle and Karlskoga but the enormous cost and the natural dourness of the Swedes had kept Grand Prix away for a long time. The usual circuits were little more than glorified club tracks so a new venue had to be conjured into being.

Anderstorp wasn't everyone's idea of a race circuit. In fact it was a bit of a setback after all the work that had been put in around the world to satisfy the demands of the Grands Prix Drivers' Association. The Swedish circuit was marked out on a tarmac runway at the airport and that was that. The townspeople weren't exactly happy to find themselves inundated with a couple of hundred or so people from different countries who were all bound solidly together in the village of Grands Prix motor racing and expected the area they were in to conform to the pattern of life they had forged for themselves. Towns with a longer association with motor racing don't find the invasion so startling. They accept it and make a lot of money out of the expense account society. Anderstorp just didn't seem able to cope and the atmosphere between the invaders and the Home Guard developed into trench warfare before the low-lying sun slipped horizonward.

Our arrival only just avoided being traumatic. After landing we made for the hotel. A few weeks previously we had gone to the Formula 2 race at, I think, Kinekulle. For some reason we had gone on an SAS flight which cost us an arm and a leg. There had been compensations; Monica for instance. Monica was in the best tradition of the Swedish breed. She was tall, blonde and beautiful. On the plane over I knocked myself out trying to foster a wonderful, lasting relationship. It got as far as a promise to attend the Formula 2 race on Sunday. That was enough to build on, so I was waiting eagerly at the appointed trysting place and escorted Monica to the track. That's where I discovered that the pecking order can be very painful. Graham hadn't shown a lot of interest in Monica on the plane; probably under the mistaken impression that all Swedish women were as

Left *The Shadow did not come up to expectations and caused a lot of reflection.*

beautiful, if not more so. This is a common mistake. All the really fantastic
Swedes seem to float around the foreign capitals of the world while those who
stay at home have a disturbing tendency to be 'homely'. Whatever the reason,
Monica made sure she wasn't overlooked at the circuit. She crouched for hours
on the pit counter giving Graham the full, hero-worshipping treatment from
hubcap-sized, limpid blue eyes. After the race I was tolerated because I had the
access but there was no mistaking where her mark was set. I fought a sullen
rearguard action and managed to spoil the fun but I wasn't exactly being voted a
runaway winner in the popularity stakes.

So there we were, back in Sweden a couple of weeks later. This time Bette had
come along as she usually did for the European Grands Prix. As we entered the
hotel there was a little whinnie of pleasure from one of the big leather chairs
dotted around the foyer and a gold crested figure reared up and surged towards
us. I say 'us', but really it was Graham. I happened to be walking between
Graham and Bette. Graham was quicker than I to spot the identity of the
marauder and with the dexterity that had made him a winner on the track he was
equal to the situation. He was on my left and Bette on my right. Monica, for
that's who I at last identified it to be, was closing at a high rate of knots on our
starboard bow, arms spread, teeth glistening like a line of lasers. 'Ah!' Graham
said, in an authoritative voice, barging me forward on an intercepting course,
'This is a friend of Tone's,' and quickly, before a denial could be mounted,
'Monica, meet my wife Bette.' Monica wasn't very convincing and did for my
ego as much good as a bucket of boiling water does for a frozen lettuce. We didn't
see her around much after that, but a few weeks later I did get a letter from

her—asking me how she could get in touch with Graham. It's one of those things that the poor racing drivers have to suffer.

At Albi later that year for a Formula 2 race there were actually young girls sitting on the steps of the prestigious Hostellerie de St Antoine and they weren't collecting autographs. The Albi race was really the last time Graham had an opportunity to relax. It was a small, no-account race on a basically safe circuit that he had competed on many times before. His appearance there with other star drivers was a cosmetic job to try to reclaim some of its former lustre when aces like Fangio, Hawthorn, Gonzalez and Moss raced there.

One of Graham's party-pieces was the crème caramel trick. At a drop of a napkin he would demand a crème caramel and, carefully primping his 'tash out of the way and checking to see that his underslung jaw wasn't going to get in the line of attack, suck up the caramel in an operation that had the delicacy of sound of a suction pump cleaning out the last dregs of a cesspit. Determined to get our own back for the times we had to suffer the exhibition, I slipped into the kitchen and had a word with the chef. Sure enough when time for pudding came Graham demanded a crème caramel. He didn't twitch a whisker when the chef, followed by the sous chef and the rest of the kitchen hierarchy, appeared, proudly carrying a crème caramel moulded in a pudding basin and weighing in at the equivalent of a litre. Watched by the rest of the amazed diners Graham drew in a deep breath and plunged into the cold custard. He tried hard. Slurping, grunting and gasping he managed to suck in three quarters of the goo before it defeated him and he slumped back in his chair, face and the front of his shirt an obscene yellow mess.

Understandably he didn't feel like going to bed after that, so we decided to go

Left *The 'hokey-cokey' with the London Festival Ballet before a charity performance of Sleeping Beauty in 1973.*

Right *Looking for a new way to the top. Graham tackles the mountains of the Massif Central.*

for a walk around the town. 'We' being actor Keith Smith, bob-sleigh and racing car driver Robin Widdows, Graham and myself. Bette decided that she had had enough entertainment for one evening and went to bed. We finished up in a bar that was hosting, in one of the upstairs rooms, a reunion of the recently excommunicated OAS. They were a pretty maudlin lot telling each other what great guys they had all been when they were bringing the graces of Paris to Algiers. They pepped up a bit when they saw Graham, and before long we were all caught up in a singing, dancing, drinking party that momentarily seemed to be on the brink of something more painful. We thought that the moment had come and edged nervously towards the door just after the umpteenth toast to someone who could obviously rouse a lot of passion in a OAS breast but meant nothing to us although we *santé'd* with the best of them. Robin Widdows, now brimming with bonhomie and *vin ordinaire*, grabbed one of the kepi-type uniform caps from a chair, stuck it on his head and advanced to the centre of the room in a fair imitation of General Charles de Gaulle. Dramatically he waited until the only sound was the creak of the floor-boards as Graham, Keith and I eased towards the door and then he flung his arms out in a florid latin gesture and said: *'Mes enfants, aprez moi—le deluge!'* There was a nasty silence and we were about to abandon him to his fate and flee the scene when there was a bellow of laughter and the ex-OAS men crowded around pressing more drinks on us and saying all sorts of funny things in French which were beyond our comprehension. Knowing when enough was enough, Graham suggested we got going. Back in the street we found that Robin hadn't been content with risking our hides once, he was now lining us up for the abbatoire again. Somehow he had managed to get out of the café with one of the soldiers' caps, which he now insisted on wearing as we walked along the street. We didn't need any urging when Graham led the way back to the hotel at a fast pace.

After Albi there didn't seem to be a lot more fun. Graham was still dedicated to golf as a way to keep his legs motivated to put in a few strenuous walking miles each week, but even these were quite dour, introspective outings as he stomped from divot to divot with none of the boyish banter of yesteryear. The problems were coming at him thick and fast and the additional problem was that he couldn't show it. By far and away the greatest blot on his copybook was the performance, or rather lack of performance, of the Shadows. Don Nichols was beginning to emulate the name of his cars and be hard to pin down. He was having his own problems, not only with his sponsors, but from within his own team, particularly with the taciturn Alan Rees and the vociferous Jack Oliver. Rees has been a reasonably able racing driver himself and had run the highly successful Winkelmann Formula 2 team with the dynamic Austrian race ace Jochen Rindt as co-driver. He wasn't used to having any car he was managing lurking dyspeptically at the tail end of the field. Oliver didn't like the embarrassment of being there either and he was beginning to flex his muscles. American George Follmer didn't seem to have an opinion but gave his share of problems. With all this going on around him, plus Graham constantly trying to tear the Shadow team apart in an effort to get some results and please his sponsor,

Nichols could do little but hunch his shoulders and pray for the end of the season.

In desperation Graham looked around the scene to see where he could forge an alliance that would work a miracle. It wasn't easy. Finding all avenues to a brighter future blocked by his affluent sponsor's suspicion of any small-time organisations, Graham looked to former glories and came up with Lola. Lola had at one time or another done everything. You could not turn to a section of the sport which hadn't, at some time, felt the crushing expertise of the Lola factory. The trouble was that they hadn't been in Grands Prix for over a decade and there were fears they might not be able to keep up with the new developments abroad. This is a problem when you are talking to sponsors about hundreds of thousands of pounds. Hill managed to do an 'all things being equal' deal on the basis of Lola's exemplary record in sports cars and recent experience in Formula 2. He would, ideally have liked something better but time was getting short and he had to have a New Year deal or be stuck with Hobson's choice of Shadow or nothing. On the brighter side, Lola offered Graham a lot of the assets which he had forgone when setting up his own team. In the Lola company he would not only be in the position of being able to bring in a fair amount of contemporary coinage but would also have the opportunity to bring Lola into the main ring. It should mean that in designing and running his team he would have a free hand. Any trepidation he might have felt about putting himself in the front line automatically took second place to the necessity to keep body and soul soaring in his high-flying social life. As these things tend to do when they first blast off, everything went swimmingly at first. Graham was even able to indulge in the luxury of a back-up driver and an extra car.

Chapter 7

Paper it's written on

While all this was going on, the scene around Graham was being captured on film by film producer Tony Maylam. The film was to be called 'Graham' and Tony wandered around the tracks picking up background stories and chat to try to nail down the character and charisma of his star. It wasn't easy, not the personal part at any rate. Graham was well known for not taking lightly any comment that might be less than complimentary. Bette had found a way to cope over the years but it was too much trouble for most people to constantly edit what they were about to say. However, when Tony Maylam went around the village asking for comments on the Hill character he was met with a bland barrage of clichés and the sort of comment usually indulged in by small boys when they know the headmaster's listening. In desperation Maylam begged interviewees to let their hair down but Graham had been around a long time and trained his acquaintances well. It was a shame really, because adverse criticism would have brought out the strong points of his character instead of painting in a figure too good to be true. Of course, much as Maylam tried, it was impossible to capture the full flavour of the excitement and emotions of that small band which haunted the circuits of the world from early January to November. But it was a good try.

The year closed on a low note, not just for Hill but for everyone who enjoyed motor racing. Jackie Stewart had squirrelled away enough points to take his third world championship before the cars were shipped to Watkins Glen in upstate New York for the last race of the 1973 season. This was always a funny race. Everyone felt they should enjoy it but somehow it always fell short of expectations. It was hardly the organisers' fault. They entered into the occasion with the sort of open enthusiasm which only Americans seem to be able to stoke up and maintain. There was a golf tournament with practically everyone who entered getting some sort of prize. Circuit parties after practice and formal celebrations were held later. There was plenty of enthusiastic help from the eager young and the not so young who, to a man or woman, called you 'sir'. Why the atmosphere didn't come across is a mystery.

In the evening the streets were lined with the sort of characters usually associated with *Woodstock* or Peter Fonda's *Easy Rider*. Everywhere there was the slightly decayed tang of marijuana and huddled in corners were dark bundles

Right *Hill signals his intentions before the start of the 1973 Grand Prix in Watkins Glen.*

who had taken something harder or were just heavy sleepers. Threading their way through this noisy, colourful invasion were the cops. Even at night these menacing, slightly corpulent figures with their heavy gun-belts cutting into them, wore sunglasses, most of them with a mirror effect. These cops seemed to have studied method acting under Rod Steiger and relied on their mirror glasses and gum-chomping jaw to do their talking for them. There was a second, leaner lot, usually older, who looked as if they had strayed from the public library. They were different. They wore gold-rimmed sunglasses, never seemed to stop talking in a sarcastic Jimmy Stewart voice, and poked anything pokable with their nightsticks. They also seemed a lot quicker to haul offenders off to gaol.

The circuit on the edge of the small town wound through a hilly piece of afforestation that in autumn must be one of the most beautiful pieces of woodland in the world. It is part of the beauty of New York State, the Fall colours of the trees spanning out around the shores of the hundreds of 'Finger Lakes' scattered throughout the area. Graham had reached the heights and plumbed the depths in Watkins Glen. It was the scene of some of his greatest triumphs and his deepest despairs. Since 1962 he had won the race three times in consecutive years and been in the frame three times more. And then there was the race in 1969 which had ended with him in Elmira Hospital with legs so badly smashed that it was feared that he would never walk again. 1973 was going to be another year that caused Graham Hill a good deal of distress. During practice François Cevert crashed the Tyrrell he was driving and it turned over and slid along the barriers, killing the young Frenchman. Graham was visibly shaken by the event. The Hills had been very friendly with the Ceverts and it seemed to affect Graham even more than when his best friend, Jo Bonnier, had been killed the year before in Le Mans as Graham won. Jackie Stewart was in no doubt as to what he should do. He withdrew from the race and went home. Shortly afterwards he announced his retirement. Graham wrestled with a problem. He felt like at least giving the race a miss. If he had put down one or two good results in the year he would probably have felt able to walk away. As it was he had put in a year for nothing and he felt he owed his sponsor something. But 1974 was going to be better!

The competitors for the vacant 1974 Embassy seat didn't exactly fit the mould of 'young talented' drivers promised the illuminating mantle of Hill tutelage. The names bandied about had all seen more exciting days. Tim Schenken from Australia, home-grown son of a champion jockey, Peter Gethin, and Howden Ganley, a lugubrious New Zealander, seemed to be favourites. Schenken was still touched by the lustre of his 'Golden Boy' label which he had acquired in the hurly-burly of Formula 3. His potential had never been reached in Formula 2 and he was still looking for the right pedal in Grands Prix. Gethin was a stayer. He had been around for a long time and had made his mark in Formula 5000 as well as putting in very respectable performances in Formula 2 and sports car racing. His staying powers had hit paydirt at Monza in 1972 when he had been on hand to take the chequered flag when more able drivers had outfumbled themselves at the final corner. In the same mould but with less experience was Ganley. At that time he hadn't separated his interest in the nuts and bolts of the game from his interest in being a competitor. He had done quite a lot of Grand Prix driving, mainly in the BRM, but didn't impress as the sort to become mercurial and rise under the Embassy wand. There was also the suspicion that Graham wasn't exactly overjoyed at the prospect of running a second car and risking a situation where his times would be open to direct comparison with another's. The ultimate competitor, he was not altruistic enough to nurture a 'viper' in his own team. But again there were the sponsors to consider. They wanted a good turn-out. They had now taken a firm grip on the nose and plunged, feet first, into the PR pool. The Embassy decals and stickers proliferated everywhere, threatening the supremacy of the Marlborough colours, which they resembled, and giving the more established JPS market a run for it's money. Where they were at a disadvantage was on the track. With only one car crawling around at the back of the field, they reckoned they weren't getting value for their support. The pressure to produce a better and more prominent turn pushed Graham into a corner. Ideally he would have preferred to wait a little until he had sorted out the new cars and then take on a back up car that was just a mobile advertisement. That's when Guy Edwards moved in.

Edwards, a psychology graduate, had applied his academic talent to winkling out sponsors. A tenacious and competitive driver in sportscar racing and Formula 5000, he had never been called upon to express himself in the more esoteric field of Grands Prix. While it was generally acknowledged that he had a good deal of natural talent, the *aficionados* claimed that he was not going to get anywhere while he spent too much of his time chasing deals and dividing his energy between getting the backing and driving. What no one else came up with was a solution to the dilemma. Edwards would have been happy to concentrate on the track ahead, without worrying what the financiers would say if he wrote off the machinery. But, until that happy day, he preferred to push further and further into the jungle of advertising in the quest for continued employment. In his continual sifting of possibilities he had come up with a likely source of funds in the petrol giant AMOCO. They were making all the right noises and Guy was happy to offer his services. After the initial *pas de deux* he was told that AMOCO were interested but couldn't be more positive until an actual, on the grid deal had been put to them. Graham's luke-warm seach for a number two was no secret and it took only a superficial glance through the other, more established teams, to see that the possibilities were limited.

So in late November 1973 Edwards put out tentative feelers in Hill's direction. When he mentioned the possibility of AMOCO coming in for about £25,000 Graham's interest quickened considerably and he invited Edwards to dinner. The basis for an agreement was knocked out and Guy reported back to his potential sponsors. They seemed delighted. Although Graham was committed to Embassy, the benefits of the association of AMOCO with a team headed by the doyen of Grands Prix drivers was not lost on their PR director. A couple of weeks before Christmas Graham rang Guy and told him he wanted to see him, in Vallelunga—a circuit just outside Rome. Excited by the prospect of a drive, Edwards arrived hotfoot at the circuit. On the way down he had imagined the historic meeting with his hero and the thrill of taking out the new car and putting it through its paces at the tight, tricky circuit. The reality was somewhat different. Testing hadn't been going too well and Graham was not at his sweetest. With only a nod and a few perfunctory words to acknowledge Edwards' presence, he spent the rest of the day searching for a more crisp performance from the Lola. Edwards hung around trying to convey absorbed interest but getting no feedback until late in the afternoon.

Graham heaved himself out of his car, took off battle-bowler and gauntlets and made it obvious that as far as he was concerned the day was over. Guy stood, stiff-faced, trying to decide what he should do. He had admired Graham for years and stood in considerable awe of his reputation. The chance to drive in the same team was a beacon to his ambition. He was about to speak when Hill became aware of him. As he walked to his car he told Ray Brimble, his chief mechanic, to let Edwards take the Lola out for a few laps to see how he felt about it.

Back in London, a few days later, Edwards got the AMOCO people together with Graham. They were still keen on the idea and brought along designs and suggestions of how they could blend in with the Embassy sponsorship. Graham warmed even more to the project. Although getting considerably more funding than he had done in his previous year he was still desperately short of capital for building, workshop equipment and all the basics that had been overlooked in the first enthusiastic cigarette packet estimate. A few days later, on Christmas Eve, Guy dropped in at Lyndhurst on his way north to Liverpool to see his parents. Graham was in an ebullient mood, freed from the cares of his hot-house existence by the moratorium that settles over England at Christimas time. Before Guy had left to continue his journey, Graham grasped his hand and gave him the Christmas present he had been saving. After due consideration and consultation with the Embassy marketing people it had been decided to offer Edwards the drive in the second Embassy Lola. With the Argentinian Grand Prix only a couple of weeks away there wouldn't be much time for him to test the car, but what did he care? The drive to Liverpool was strictly cloud nine. The couple of days left of the festive season went by in a whirl. As soon as he decently could Edwards rang AMOCO and told them of Graham's decision. Their reply brought Christmas to a close with a crashing discord. After due consideration they had decided not to enter into the perilous world of motor racing sponsorship!

Dreading the confrontation, Edwards made his way back to Lyndhurst. He was quite aware of the fact that the drive had been offered more to the potential currency notes in the bank than to him as a driver. Predictably Graham was not pleased. He had already allocated the windfall finance that his new protégé would bring. Edwards could do nothing but backtrack with apologies and promise to try to come up with an alternative as speedily as possible. As he drove back to his Chelsea apartment he said goodbye to the prospect of a couple of weeks in the southern hemisphere. He had hardly fed the cat when the telephone rang and Graham told him that the deal was still on. Guy restated his determination to find

Right *Definitely not just a pretty face.*

Wilson

new sponsorship and after he hung up, he felt like ringing back to check that it was all true and he hadn't got the wrong end of the stick. Come what may, he now looked set to combat the world championship in Formula 1 for the next two years.

A few days later he was off to Buenos Aires. Graham had a colossal following in Argentina and Edwards was practically overlooked in the Press rush to Hill's door. That suited the Liverpudlian. He was just happy to drive around in the new Lola and hoped to play himself in without too much trauma. The Admiral Brown circuit was just the right place to do it. Big and open, with large stretches of flat run-off area all around, it gave drivers the opportunity to test their car to the limit without fear of hitting something immovable. As he flashed around the green oasis in the blazing sunlight Edwards couldn't believe his luck. His gratitude to Graham was total but the team boss wasn't looking for tail wagging. He still wasn't getting the performance he wanted and the public adulation and the snide local Press comments were getting to him. Edwards proved a convenient whipping boy. Their relationship soured rapidly over a trivial piece of thoughtlessness. The Edwards' helmet had a white space in front. A convenient bill-board for advertising and one used by AMOCO when they were outlining their special requirements. Edwards had offered it to Graham but had been told to hold it for the moment and see what sort of deal could be done for it outside the realm of the current sponsorship. Then the Embassy PR men suggested to Guy that he should stick a decal in the vacant space.

The weather was hot and gruelling and Graham was suffering. The Embassy decal enblazoned above Edwards' eyebrows sparked off the detonation. Normally Hill would have made a passing, sarcastic remark and that would have been the end of the matter. In the circumstances it became a plague spot which had to be eradicated. Edwards got the full venom of Graham's pent up frustration. Chastened, Guy dropped the decal he had obligingly worn, but the incident was a thorn which lay beneath the surface, ready to prick when inadvertently pressed.

The next race at Interlagos in Brazil was the same only more so. Although the steamy Buenos Aires heat had been pretty overpowering, it was relieved by cool nights, green trees and the regular fortnightly cloudburst. Around Sao Paolo there were no such saving graces. It was just hot, hotter and hottest. The enclosed bodywork of the Lola, with its spectacular, sail-like ram-air box wasn't built for the climate. As it slogged around on the griddle-hot tarmac it suffered, with unnerving regularity, all the little annoying ailments that beset a new and unsorted car. Worse still, the Edwards car was having the temerity to out-perform the one driven by the boss. The static charged atmosphere of the tortuously writhing circuit, surrounded by thousands of excitable *mariachi* exponents isn't the most tranquil place. Stir in a prying, provoking Press and the ignition is primed. Exotic food and hygiene standards that would stop Egon Ronay in his tracks were also adding to the agitation.

To be truthful it wasn't just the Embassy team which was having a bad time. Their fellow purveyors of tobacco, Marlboro, were also coming in for some criticism. At a big 'Welcome to Sao Paolo' party held in the Hilton hotel and then moving off to a venue on the outskirts of the city, they were receiving the backlash resulting from their sycophantic courtship of the world's Press. Bernard Cahier, the dictatorial leader of the Internation Racing Press Association, was being pettish because he hadn't even been asked to hand out the monthly prizes to deserving journalists and drivers. It caused a lot of skulking and scowling, with the scribes split between gleeful merriment at Cahier's discomfiture and a feeling that they should stand solidly shoulder to shoulder in the face of the erosion of their rights. Some of the journalists remembered the farce the year before at the Austrian Grand Prix and preferred to stay aloof. Then there had been a call for solidarity and a sit-down strike in the pit lane to prevent practice starting. It was all to do with Press passes, or the non-existence of them, and had been reduced to a shambles by Clay Regazzoni's acceleration down the pit lane, with the obvious intention of settling a few scores for unflattering comments over the years. Sao Paolo stood a good chance of being the theatre for another débâcle.

Amongst all the muttering and shuffling Graham was being magnificent. Mindful of his rating in the 'Best Dressed Man' stakes, and welcoming the chance to exemplify the 'mad dogs and Englishmen' syndrome, he was beautifully kitted out in an expensively tailored silk suit, Lanvin tie and Gieves shirt. At first glance he appeared to be relaxed and urbane, until you got close and could see the restless flick of his hooded eyes and the unnatural stillness of his face muscles as he waited for the opportunity to slip a polished steel barb into the conversation. He was at his evil best, cutting through the barrage of trivia like a buccaneer. When it was announced that we were about to move on to the main part of the evening, Graham called me across and asked if I had a car. Reluctantly I confessed I had. I knew what was coming but couldn't think of a way to head it off. 'Right,' he said, 'we'll take your car and then we can sod off when we want to.' I protested weakly that I didn't know the way, but he wasn't going to be put off by that. The organisers offered to lay on a car for him but he waved that aside. All he wanted was the address of the party. Someone gave it to him and he thrust it in my hand and stalked off.

In the lift to the ground floor there was an uncomfortable silence. Several other passengers recognised Graham but luckily they also recognised the signals he was sending out and didn't try to communicate. As we left the lift I told Graham that the address didn't help a lot if we didn't know where it was we were going. He flared his nostrils and made a noise in the back of his throat, then swung around and marched off to the hall porter's desk. There was a big negro resplendent in a semi-military uniform and standing behind the desk. He wasn't smiling either. Graham slammed the piece of paper on the desk in front of him. 'Where is this place?' he demanded. I tried a conciliatory smile but was ignored. With a finger that looked like a pink-tipped over-ripe banana, the hall-porter turned the paper round and gave it the sort of attention usually seen in betting shops before a big race. Graham shifted impatiently from foot to foot and I leaned over as if a demonstration of intentness would be illuminating. Finally the big man pushed the paper back, pointed out of the door and spoke in a fair imitation of Quarrel in *Dr No*.

'You take de lef' ontu de car park, and swivel a hard-on right. Then you take in about fo'-five blocks and turn on to de straightaway goin' on to de town. . .'

His colourful directions were cut short by Graham who was getting meaner by the minute. 'Write it down,' he snarled, and bowled off. It was the first time I had seen him walking from a distance. I realised that he was limping. If he was limping it meant he was in considerable pain. He made it a principle of life to hide any discomfort he was feeling. It was a declaration that he was less then perfect and it made him feel vulnerable. In the car I looked at the drawing the porter had made of the route. I wished I hadn't been so distracted by Graham's limp. It was obviously going to be one of those journeys.

As we set off through the chaotic jungle of Volkswagen Beetles that make up 99 per cent of Brazil's traffic, I ventured a question about Graham's leg. He shrugged his shoulders and struck the offending knee angrily. Evidently he had struck it on the side of his Lola as he was getting out and must have compressed one of the strangled nerve ends in his patchwork leg. We hadn't gone a couple of blocks when it was self-evident that we were hopelessly lost. Savagely Graham swung to the kerb and frostily took the map from my hand. I tried to explain, from a font of navigational ignorance, where we were, but he wasn't listening. Silently he swung the car around and set off back the way we had come. The Hilton has a driveway that sweeps up under a covered way. In front are a number of tables and chairs. On this occasion these were filled with drivers and mechanics watching the beautiful colourful Brazilian women parading their wares on the pavement below. As Graham screeched to a halt and struggled from the car there were a few ribald remarks thrown his way. They fell on stoney ears as he strode purposefully through the doors into the foyer, leaving the car door open and me wondering what to do next. I guessed I was on my own so I rescued

A good time was had by all! Graham's 45th birthday, and, at Lyndhurst to celebrate, Vicky and David Mason, Henry and Albina Cooper and Doreen and Ernie Wise.

Colin Chapman being presented with the Alfred Neubauer Trophy by Neubauer himself, 1974.

the piece of paper from the floor and looked up the hall-porter again. All was rapidly revealed. The first left and right, which I had taken to be roads, were in fact walking across the foyer, turning left outside the revolving doors and then right out on to the road. He smiled as he explained and I had the feeling that he was marking up a mental score. Graham wasn't in the lobby or in either of the bars so I rang his room. His response was short and to the point. No, he wasn't going on safari again. It was probably just as well. The party turned out to be pretty dramatic. Cahier engineered a walk-out of committed journalists and then a fight broke out and threatened to develop into a free-for-all. At the circuit the following morning Graham seemed to have recovered a little of his equanimity although there was a lack of communication between him and Edwards.

Off the circuit the Hill/Edwards alliance rubbed along without much friction. Guy was still a fan of the ex-World Champion and considered that Graham had acted pretty well over the non-appearance of the AMOCO sponsorship deal. If his inclusion in the team wasn't all that the *Boys Own Paper* might have portrayed he wasn't complaining. He was in a number one team, contesting international Grands Prix with a comforting two year contract tucked safely away in his Nomex to add to his commitment to a Formula 5000 season. Life was good! In the shade from the great man's shadow he was able to beaver away learning his trade and stowing away a potful of honey for another and less salubrious day.

Graham was busier than ever. For years now he had been canvassing for a better deal for the disabled. He hadn't pulled any punches in his condemnation of the motorised tricycle which had been developed with little thought for the needs of the driver. Graham's spell in plaster in 1969 had made him highly sensitive to what was needed and at last he was near to winning the day and having the dangerous 'trike' relegated to the museum. He was also having a flirtation with the 'Yellow Perils'—the traffic wardens. In an attempt to sell their services to a hostile public, Ambassador Hill had been called in to lead the be-kind-to-traffic-wardens rally. Even Graham, in his more reflective moments, admitted that he was taking on too much. But he didn't know how to cut down and sort out which invitation, out of hundreds, to accept.

By now Graham had shed his long-term manager, Lister Welsh, in favour of a cobbled together relationship with Mark McCormack. The deal was typical of Graham's growing disorientation on something as basic as this. Coming late in life to the responsibility of living from day to day without a sheltering umbrella, he was finding the going hard. His answer was the one he invariably used, with success, on the track. He matched aggression with aggression, argument with argument, force with force. Unfortunately, he was finding that it didn't work quite that way in other spheres. As team boss he was where the buck stopped. Prepared to accept the responsibility, he was nevertheless ill-equipped to cope with it. De Cadinet could have coped, and Guy Edwards, given the opportunity, would have been an invaluable ally. To Graham it was all coming at him too fast, not giving him time to sort out his priorities. The best ploy at that point would have been to dump his personal future in the lap of McCormack, get in an experienced team manager, get his faithful aid, Gabrielle, to edit ruthlessly his public appearances and get on with the job to which he was eminently suited— Ambassador of Motor Racing. Instead he got himself even more involved in the political wrangles of the GPDA of which he had now superseded Denny Hulme as President.

McCormack allowed him to patch up an agreement which meant that Graham was still on the hook for the UK side of the operation. At first it seemed to be working but just as a gleam appeared in the darkness, Guy Edwards broke a bone in his wrist in a Formula 5000 shunt. This didn't make him the most popular driver in Nomex. Although Graham had been doing his best to forget the unfortunate start to their relationship, he seemed to categorise the new crisis under the military heading 'self inflicted injury'. It was probably brought about by the new thinking in Grands Prix racing that it was a discipline apart and should not be sullied by other, less refined forms of the art. As a driver Graham had thought just the opposite. In a week he would sometimes take part in a rally, drive in a saloon car, sports car, Formula 2 or 1 race and throw in a midget or lawn mower race for good measure. As a manager he looked upon any activity which might deplete the strength of his team as an unnecessary evil. Besides, a simple fracture of the arm seemed almost too trivial to mention. The thick plaster of Paris casing would absorb any pressure. Edwards felt chagrined that just when his career was set to go places he was making excuses.

Reluctantly Hill agreed that Edwards could sit the British Grand Prix out and brought in Brands Hatch favourite Peter Gethin for the race. Niki Lauda dominated the race and was fumbled out of the win at the end after coming into the pits for a tyre change. When he tried to get back on to the circuit the exit from the pit lane was blocked by a herd of racing groupies and the attendant 'Hooray Henrys' that the British Grand Prix brings out of the clubs and pubs. The resulting fiasco, involving protests and the blue-blazered hierarchy of the Royal Automobile Club, helped to divert attention from the miserable showing of London's favourite racers, Hill and Gethin. This was just as well, because after just scraping in at the tail end of the field the race was something both would rather forget.

Under pressure, Guy Edwards agreed to try out the crippled wing for the next race at the tortuous 22 k Nürburgring in the Eiffel mountains of West Germany. As a precaution he suggested to Graham that Peter Gethin should be standing by to take over if the going got too tough. It didn't take long to find out that he was in a no-go situation. A couple of tentative circuits hurt, but not enough to warrant intensive care, so Edwards decided to try a quick lap. The cast made it impossible to use his wrist for any delicate work, so he was using his sound arm mainly and risking his injured arm as an auxiliary, until he hit *Flugplatz*. As he lifted off and glided several feet above the tarmac he realised that he had reached the moment of truth. To keep the car in line he was going to need all his strength as the wheels hit terra firma. He tried to keep the load on the good wrist but it was not strong enough for the job and needed back-up support. As he applied pressure to the steering wheel to get back in line the pain that shot through his body made him exclaim into the sound-proof box of his helmet. As soon as he got the Lola back under control he slowed up and motored back to the pit. Graham was out on the circuit at the time but when he got back and found that his co-driver had quit he made no bones about what he thought of him. When Guy tried to defend himself by reminding his boss that he had told him to have a back-up driver in attendance, he was treated with scorn. A racing driver didn't quit in the middle of practice unless he was a stretcher case.

The relationship was all up-hill after that. The bespectacled German driver, Rolf Stommelen was brought in to fill the gap for the next race at Zeltweg in Austria while Guy Edwards nursed his injury. It was a bit of a surprise as previous publicity had made a big issue of the 'British' nature of the Embassy team. And again Rolf wasn't a driver who was particularly noted for youth and genius. He had been around for a long time and made a bit of a name for himself in sports car racing but there were plenty of more obvious prospects. There were four more races that season and Edwards was not unhappy with the choice of his temporary replacement. If it had been one of the pushy young lions on the way up he would have been worried. Overtly the Edwards/Hill partnership was still extant. Graham was heavily involved in team management and establishing his fame with a rapidly expanding public while Edwards was being generally helpful and comradely from the sidelines. There were the odd moments of panic. Like when a rumour floated around the paddock linking Hill, Stommelen, Lola and

Alfa Romeo. Rumours are common in motor racing, particularly at the fag-end of the season and, sensibly, Edwards ignored the irritating bit of intelligence. He had a two-year contract, signed and sealed, and he was astute enough to know the difference between a firm covenant and wallpaper.

Hill and Stommelen got on well together, Rolf preferring to stay out of the politics and mechanics and stick with the body-building and tennis. The Lolas were at last staying in one piece and were beginning at least to get the outfall of Champagne sprayed from the winners' rostrum. The last three races were quite exciting, with Hill taking a couple of eighth places, just outside the store of championship points, and Stommelen doing a stirring job as back-up man. The favourite sporting headlines were still in the vein of 'Over the Hill' and 'Hill to retire' but the squire was still in there hunting for a return to form which would confound the critics and fortify the over forties. It was asking a bit much of the ex-mechanic, who had forced himself from the era of Fangio and Moss, into the world of cheque-book racing.

As if having to carry the burden of his years wasn't enough he had also saddled himself with a car that, although proving reliable and finishing the season with a reliability factor of over 70 per cent (a standard unknown in Formula 1 before), was basically a hash-up from a less sophisticated formula, Formula 5000, and carried enough excess weight to keep it firmly out of the high-flying front runners clique.

Graham was discussing the new slim-line model—which was to bring the Lola connection to a close and give birth in 1975 to the new marque to be known as the Embassy-Hill—with his chief mechanic at their chicken-coop headquarters at Feltham, when Guy Edwards learned the unpalatable truth. Stoically ignoring the persistent rumours that a Hill/Stommelen link had now been forged, Edwards dropped into the workshop to discuss his seating requirements in the new car. Hill called him into the office. He didn't beat around the bush. It was the sort of situation that few relish and Graham less than most. In a few words he thanked Guy for his support and told him that his services wouldn't be required for the coming year and would he shut the door on the way out, please. Edwards was stunned. It was a recurring fear that had been with him for some time now but the bald statement left him speechless. He tried to point out that he had a contract but Graham, brought up under Colin Chapman in the belief that verbal contracts weren't worth the paper they were written on, and dismissing the inconvenient fact that Edwards' contract was a written one, wasn't interested.

Edwards drove back to London in despair. It seemed that his promise of Grands Prix honours had been dashed before he had been able to run the seat of his pants in. What chance had he got at that late stage of finding another team willing to take on a driver, new to Grands Prix, who had been thrown out of his first team after completing only half a season and was known as a character who spent more time in accountants' offices than he did on the track? He saw his lawyer and a few days later Graham received a letter stating that either he took up Edwards' contract or paid him for loss of earnings. It was Hill's turn to be dumbfounded. In his 20 odd years of racing he had never been thrown a curve

Right *The spacious grounds of his garden at Shenley provided a chance for Graham to keep his hand in at scrambling.*

Below *German Rolf Stommelen in the driving seat of the Embassy Lola T371 and Hill acting as team manager at the Race of Champions at Brands Hatch, 1975.*

like this. One expected the Italians or the Argentinians to get messy and throw summonses around if someone got axed on one of their circuits, but they were mainly of Latin extraction and hadn't the phlegm of the 'True Brit'. If it were taken seriously it would be the beginning of the end. Magnificently Hill ignored it and concentrated on what he was more familiar with—the cars. This was a pity since initially it is possible that a reasonable deal could have been done and some of the acrimony that later arose could have been avoided completely.

Apart from more immediate matters, the one dominating topic in 1975 was the oil crisis. It had been dragging on since the year before, when it had been touch and go whether motor racing would survive. The energy-saving lobby shrieked loudly about the criminal waste of natural resources, while the vested interests pointed out that it took less fuel to run a year's motor racing than it did to fly a Jumbo jet from London to New York. As with most precipitate statements, it tended to inflame rather than heal the breach in relations. Graham kept his head down on this one and refused to be baited into making a statement. Instead he diverted attention to his increasing involvement with the Royal Family and the county set he shot with. It was a poor boy's dream. Clad in his Norfolk tweeds and flat hat he stomped across the heaths in the footsteps of the similarly attired Prince of Wales and armed nobles of lesser rank. On the co-ordination necessary to close the wings of a partridge in full flight, topping 60 miles an hour, he waxed long and lyrical. The subject even inched out his golf stories.

One of the most creditable aspects of Graham's character was his restraint in circumstances where names could easily be dropped. He was the soul of discretion in this context. Everybody knew that he was on hob-nobbing terms with the Mountbattens and Brabournes and had confided many a *risqué* story to the heir to the throne but he never, ever, told indiscrete stories. It wasn't just that he knew that an incautious report would have him off the palace Christmas card list. He genuinely believed in keeping the facets of his multifarious existence, separate.

Although his ability at 'shooting birds up the chuff' might be improving, the golf ball still hadn't been abandoned. Graham was packed full of good advice. Practically every pro-golfer in the world had looked at his backswing and offered nuggets of wisdom. But Graham still preferred to scowl at the ball, clench his underslung jaw in determination and whack at it with his muscular arms. He believed all that was told him about swing and accelerating the club head but it all seemed to desert him at the top of his backswing. Despite this, he was happy.

He had broken the century, and even finished the game with the same ball which he had started with a couple of times. He had also gone into the design end of the game with a putter which had been sawn down to about 15 ins. As no-one has jumped on the invention and patented it there is no need to describe its effectiveness further.

Somewhere between his shooting and golfing, his driving and his management, the cost of decorating and running his mansion in Shenley and his role as a fully-fledged celebrity, the thought had lodged in his brain that maybe it was about time to put off the things of a child and get down to providing security for his old

HRH Prince Charles was a great admirer of the double World Champion. Here he asks Bette who her friend is in the line-up.

age. One possibility was a grandstand retirement in Monaco where his five phenomenal wins made him undisputed master. He had a good opportunity to get out during practice in the South African Grand Prix. At least it looked good to everyone but Hill. After he wrote off his Lola at Kyalami, and miraculously escaped without injury, an announcement was expected, but it wasn't forthcoming. It wasn't the Hill way. The 1975 Brands Hatch Race of Champions was the next race pencilled in Graham's diary but he decided to give it a miss and look after Stommelen's entry. It was the first time and he had openly made the statement that he was going to act as team manager. Before it had always been an open-ended arrangement. There was an excuse. After the pile-up in South Africa there was not enough straight metal in his race car to justify grid space so he wanted time to get it sorted out. Silverstone, he promised, would be a different matter. There the disappointed Brands Hatch fans could take the trip up the M1 and see the revival of Hill and Lola in the home of British Racing competing for the Daily Express International Trophy. But before that there was to be Spain and that morale-sapping decision about Monaco. Graham dithered. For the first time in his career he let his insecurity hang out. Earlier he would have made up his mind without reference to anybody. Suddenly he was asking leading questions about Press reaction and whether it would be better to do this or that. He knew what he was (or more correctly—wasn't) doing and it irked him. It made him even more short-tempered and abrasive in his dealings with those around him.

The beautiful but treacherous Barcelona circuit wasn't one that held happy memories for Hill. It was there in 1969, when he was co-starring with Austrian Jochen Rindt in the Lotus production, that he had survived a nasty accident in the same place that Rindt had taken a flier at the Armco barrier a few laps previously. The blame had been laid on the high-mounted wings which had proliferated throughout Formula racing in '68 and, because of the Hill/Rindt accidents, were finally taken off in 1969. Hill again made the announcement that his involvement would be purely managerial. This time he was bringing in another foreigner to fill an experimental seat, a Frenchman known more for his enthusiasm than accomplished driving skill, Francois Migault.

In his new capacity as entrant, constructor and team manager Hill worked around the clock in the days leading up to the race. What he needed was a longer day for keeping up with the demands on his time in all his trackside capacities as well as the onerous round of socialising resulting from his role as Ambassador of Motor Sport.

It wasn't an easy Grand Prix. Jody Scheckter, the South African with a title of his own in mind, didn't like the installations around the track. Badly-sited barriers were named specifically, but it was understood that Scheckter thought a typically botched job had been done by the organisers and that the GPDA should make sure that the often deferred closure of Montjuich Parque as a Grand Prix

Left *Riding wasn't Graham's thing, the face looks all right but the hand reveals insecurity.*

Right *The compleat country squire.*

Lotus 72 with the high-flying wing at the 1969 Daily Express Trophy meeting at Silverstone. It was the collapse of this wing, and that on the Rindt car in Barcelona, which was to lead to their being banned.

venue should not be delayed any longer. Emerson Fittipaldi, once a Brazilian hotshot prepared to race on a rocket-charged, radioactive skateboard if it would get him onto the grid, lent the weight of his two world championships, and also roped in Lauda who was a practised complainant. Graham, now also weighted down with the responsibility of the presidency of the GPDA, was prised away from his inquisitive probing into the entrails of his new car, much to the relief of his long-suffering mechanics, and made to walk the course and make solemn judgements when called upon to do so. James Hunt joined in because it was a hot day and it gave him a chance to walk around the circuit without his shirt on, away from the shadow of the trees. Overnight the Spanish Automobile Club called up a regiment of reserves and by the next morning Graham was able to at least shed the worry of whether the track was raceable. Undemocratically, Emerson Fittipaldi was not happy with the decision of his peers in the GPDA and failed to qualify for the grid. His Cassandra-like warnings were all too quickly affirmed, and Graham was plunged into more morale-sapping controversy and money-draining rebuilding.

The morning dawned cloudless and warm, not oppressively hot but warm enough to make the British contingent feel tropical. The crowds had been arriving for days, picking their way through the exhausted pilgrims in the plaza and struggling to maintain suicidal positions next to the barriers. Graham was making a good show of enjoying himself in the pit lane. Due to his constant exertion, the cars were ready and there was none of the last minute panic that can be so unnerving before a race. The excitement of seeing Stommelen storm into an early lead almost compensated Graham for his track-side position. Then disaster struck! The large aerofoil, built horizontally onto the rear of a car like an inverted wing to help it grip the road in the corners, broke loose. At a 150 mph the GH2 went out of control in the same spot that had taken out Hill and Rindt five years previously with the same failure. Stommelen hit the barrier, bounced back across the track, side-swiping the Brabham of Brazilian Carlos Pace, launched himself onto the top of the barrier, and slid along shedding bits of racing car like a dog drying itself after a swim. He was brought to an abrupt halt when the back of the car hit a lamp post, split in two and flipped over, leaving the German driver badly injured and dangling from his safety harness while gallons of gasoline cascaded over him and ran like a stream down the hill. When the dust and smoke cleared, five bodies lay in the wreckage that was strewn about the area; a photographer, a fire marshal and three spectators, one a teenage boy.

The Spanish reaction to the tragedy had black jokes about *mañana* on everyone's lips. Although the accident happened within a couple of hundred yards of the pits it took official help over ten minutes to arrive. First on the scene were Graham, and Emerson's big brother, Wilson. While the police and marshals milled around in a comic ballet of incompetence, these two organised spectators to get Rolf Stommelen free and try to comfort the injured and bereaved. Stommelen was unconscious and looked in a bad way. Graham had seen it all before. He had torn the metal apart with his bare hands to release Jackie Stewart trapped in his car at Spa a decade before and had only the previous year been the first into the potential bomb of Peter Revson's shattered car at Kyalami. This time it was different. He wasn't a driver in a 'them and us' situation. As an entrant, he was one of 'them' and the awful responsibility hit him hard. It came as a relief to find later that Stommelen had only two leg fractures, a smashed kneecap, cracked ribs and a broken wrist.

The spectators were a different thing. Graham wanted to do something, even if it was only to apologise. Local friends headed him off from any overt commitment, however well-meaning. It was just as well. It wasn't long before word was out that Hill was to be arraigned on a manslaughter charge as the constructor of the Embassy/Hill GH2. This was not an unknown occurrence in some countries, as Graham well knew. Jimmy Clark hadn't been able to return to Italy after being involved in the accident that killed von Trips at Monza. More recently Colin Chapman had been ducking and diving on the same charge after Jochen Rindt's accident at the same circuit. And Jean Pierre Beltoise had only just got a case against him dismissed, after three years, after being in the wrong place at the wrong time in Buenos Aires when Italian rising star Giunti fatally crashed into the back of his stalled Matra. The fear was ill-founded or at least the Spanish racing officials said it was, but Graham decided not to be caught on the hop. Having done everything he could to make sure that he wasn't wanted, he became a moving target. Peter Dyke, the Embassy PR man, kept up a mother hen front while Graham, after reassuring himself with a visit to the hospital that Stommelen was recovering, leaped aboard his Aztec and took a bearing on Elstree.

Chapter 8

The black veil

The questions most apt to cause a tightening of the jaw line, and which Graham least liked being asked were those about death. This is justifiable if you are in a business whose currencies are units of power and speed. Over the years he had seen many friends pay the price which made the legend on the entry ticket—'Motor Racing is Dangerous'—a gruesome reality. Usually a death on the track is treated like a death in the family. It is a private affair which makes outside interest seem vulgar and prying. It's a time when those most closely connected withdraw behind a black veil and resent inquisitive intruders. At these times it is hard to imagine what effect the fatality has on the survivors. In some ways there is even a sense of relief, a feeling that the odds have lengthened. At one time the statisticians worked out that there was an average of 12 deaths a year in motor racing. Another statistic put the life expectancy of a full-time racing driver at 12 years. That could sound like a long time until you think about it. There were a lot of drivers who did their time at the front and survived. Add in the maimed and the walking wounded and then take a hard look at that 12 year figure and it is less comforting. It means that a lot of drivers die early in their career to support the mathematicians' claim.

The record books support the lack of longevity amongst front line drivers. Graham watched the list grow. Ricardo Rodriguez, just 20 years of age, took the gilt off Graham's first championship year by being killed at the tail end of the season. The younger brother of Pedro, who was also to become a race track fatality ten years later, he was pushing for a good practice time in front of his home crowd in Mexico City and made an error which killed him. In the earlier, more pushy days Hill shrugged aside the tragedies. They happened to someone else. Intellectually he knew that he was someone else to someone else but the necessary self-assurance, which everyone needs to live, defeated rational argument. The crash that froze him to the spot with no possibility of side-stepping was that of his long time rival Jimmy Clark. He, like everyone who rode the razor-blade at that time, was forced to face the facts. This wasn't a young boy like Ricardo Rodriguez or a battle-weary veteran like von Trips. This was Jimmy Clark, the racer's driver, a contemporary! Fear that if he looked long enough he would put himself in Jimmy's seat, focussed Graham's attention on the job in hand. When fellow Lotus driver Mike Spence died in practice for Indianapolis a couple of months later, he kept his blinkered gaze forward.

Death became fashionable for the scribes. It always had been, but now a new generation wanted to put it under the microscope. A number of medical men got into the act with solemn treatises confirming that racing drivers either had a gigantic death wish with subjugated libido problems or were sex-mad perverts who worked out their lust on their cars. Racing drivers by and large contributed to the research only with their blood. Their reticence didn't stop the questions being asked but it did make the uncorroborated answers appear as pertinent as the latest rise in guano prices. The deaths thudded home the message. Paul Hawkins, the wise cracking practical joker from Australia wrapped his car around a tree at Oulton Park. Frenchman Jo Schlesser at Rouen bulldozed a bank and died in the blazing furnace of an unproven Honda. Then in 1970 came the triple blows of Jochen Rindt, Piers Courage and Bruce McLaren. These were tragedies which Graham faced, whatever toll they took on him mentally. He never discussed them and discouraged others from doing so in his company.

Jochen Rindt visited Graham at Elstree to take lessons in the Aztec.

Unpredictably, the death which seemed to make him want to verbalise his fears was that of Jo Siffert in a hastily promoted end-of-season race to celebrate Jackie Stewart's winning the world championship. Ironically, the reason John Webb of Brands Hatch had seen fit to slip in the extra race at the end of the year was that the GPDA had decided to boycott the Mexican Grand Prix as unsafe. The BARC was responsible for running the race under the direction of Grahame White. Although eye witnesses described a set of circumstances which would have meant that Siffert was dead before his flaming machinery smashed to a halt, later statements uncovered the can of worms which hindsight always breeds. At first sight it appeared that something had broken off Jo's BRM and as a result he had hurtled off the track at 150 mph, hit the embankment, burst into flames and finally crashed back onto the track. The first rumblings of dissent with this generally held opinion came following the publication of a picture of a fire marshal standing amongst the debris with a cigarette between his lips. Why this should be such a heinous crime was never satisfactorily explained. If it had something to do with fire hazard the outcry seems a bit specious. The wreckage of the car had been thoroughly burnt out and the petrol used up. Gradually the cricticisms became more diverse. The communications link-up to race control and the other marshal posts around the track hadn't been working one hundred per cent. Fire extinguishers also were the subject of more acrimony. A high percentage of them were found to be unserviceable when they were needed.

Graham took the opportunity to question Grahame White about the problems at Brands Hatch as we were driving to a golf match at the RAC Club at Epsom. The conversation started out fairly low-keyed. Hill asked White who was actually responsible for the serviceability of the appliances and White admitted that, as the man in charge, the onus was on him to check everything out. As a rider he added that Brands Hatch circuit must share some of the criticism as it was their gear which the organising club had to use. Hill brushed the attempt at justification aside and continued to bombard White with questions all the way to Epsom. His interest in the mechanics of the build up to a race meeting was unusual. Firmly entrenched as a works driver, he was of the opinion that everyone was as dedicated to perfection as he was. Egged on by the other drivers, he was willing to clamour for changes which increased the relatively low safety factor of an egg shell car bulleting around a circuit at nearly 200 mph with a payload of one fragile body and a fuel capacity of 40 gallons. But in spite of his intellectual awareness of the perils of his profession, it was Siffert's death which brought them home to him. Maybe it was the long wait he had in the car while the track was cleared. All the cars were forced to halt just short of the holocaust. The drivers sat and watched helplessly until the flames were brought under control and Siffert's limp, charred body finally removed. Graham had seen it all before but this time he related it to himself. The game of golf at the RAC Club wasn't a happy affair. Graham had worked himself into a black mood which even the therapeutic effect of thrashing at the little white ball was unable to lift.

A few days later Graham and I had a meeting at Esso in their luxurious offices in Victoria. We had put a proposal to them for a forecourt sales gimmick which was different and could do a lot to promote international motor racing as well as putting a comforting bulge in our hip pockets. It was the third or fourth meeting. Initial reaction had been swift and positive.

After that we kept getting asked back for more discussions which weren't getting anywhere. Graham told me to pick him up at his solicitor's office in Bedford Square. When I arrived there, it was obvious that his black mood of a couple of days before hadn't lightened much. While I sat and made a drama of time passing, Graham made loud telephone calls and dictated instructions to a secretary and anyone else who ventured within range of the open door. It was already ten minutes after the time when we should have been in Victoria when he grabbed his coat and stormed out of the office. Guessing that I either went with him without being told, or I got left behind, I hastily followed. As we pushed through the traffic he told me what a waste of time it all was and he was getting tired of always being used. That brought on a blush as it wasn't too clear who he was referring to.

In the Esso reception area we were told to wait. Graham made a sarcastic remark to the receptionist and was just about to charge out of the office after five minutes when a jolly young executive in a standard-issue blue suit arrived and made chortling, patronising remarks which he imagined revealed the depths of his bonhomie. We were ushered into a long boardroom filled with a wide, highly polished table. There was a general to-ing and fro-ing as various managers and

Moment of impact — Graham Hill in the 1969 Spanish Grand Prix at Barcelona.

executives paraded through to bid Graham welcome. As the herd cleared we were left with half a dozen well-tailored bodies around the table, smiling encouragement at an unnaturally silent ex-world champion. After coffee had been served and everybody had told Graham where they had seen him before, the senior executive raised the matter of what we were there for, basically £50,000. Various other properly shaven faces chipped in with their two pence worth at the appropriate time.

The main problem seemed to centre around the legality of our scheme. Things hinged on whether what we were selling was a game of chance (illegal) or a matter of expertise (legal). Gallantly I tried to keep up our end by running hares which would hopefully make up their minds for them that everything was above board. It is not easy to put on a good performance when you are aware that you are sitting next to 180 lb of sweating gelignite. The flash point came when one of the Esso men asked Graham what he thought. Dramatically Graham pushed himself to his feet. It was obvious that he had rehearsed this moment and it was giving him a good deal of satisfaction. 'Perhaps one of you would like to bite my ear,' he suggested lightly, an evil smile stretching his moustache. 'I like a bit of passion when I'm fucked about!' He let his smile encompass everyone in the room. 'Good afternoon,' he said and turned and walked out. It shook me. There I was with papers all over the table and my number one selling point had just planted the toe of his boot in the orifice which was supposed to spew forth gold. Compromised beyond redemption I shovelled everything in my briefcase and stumbled after Graham. As we drove past Buckingham Palace and up Park Lane neither of us said anything. For me the sudden cessation of pleasantries with the oil giant had sent me back to the position of avoiding my bank manager. We turned off and parked in Berkeley Square and Graham led the way into the Clermont Club. As we pushed through into the reception area a number of bored inmates sauntered over to try and get a comradely word from the famous man-about-town. His frozen visage told most that it wasn't a good time for banality. The few who didn't pick up the warning signals were cut to size without the elegance of the épée.

Graham found a seat in a corner and sat with his back to the room while he ordered some refreshments. I tried to school my reaction to what I expected to be an attack on me for wasting his time. Instead he asked me about a series of pen-portraits I had been doing for *Motor*. He congratulated me on the big spread I had got for Denny Hulme and asked me how the 'Bear' had reacted. He was known not to be too fond of being exposed on the written page. Thoughts of his reaction had worried me for a while. Especially when he had made a point of calling me into his pit in Zeltweg. All he had wanted to tell me was that I had got some trifling point wrong but he had seemed quite pleased with the overall result. I told Graham that. He nodded and looked as if there was something more I was supposed to add. I obliged and told him that I was hoping to do a similar job on him. It was the right offer. He had something on his chest and he was anxious to shift the weight. After some general verbiage he made sure that my tape recorder was working and opened up. I duly filed the copy but editors being what they are it was cut to pieces and very little of what he wanted to get across was left. It's worth putting in here.

After a few comments on the general atmosphere of motor racing, he got down to what he wanted to say.

'You know, it's easy for armchair *aficionados* to sit around and put everything right. Just say that this should be done or this should be avoided. The only people who lay it on the line are the drivers. They are the ones who have to go out there and contend with everyone else's mistakes. Right, I know that we don't have to drive but that's negative. If all the top drivers today said they were not going to drive until such-and-such was done—what would happen? I tell you! The Press would have a field day telling everyone how yellow we are and how all we are interested in is earning big money without taking risks. You know that's true! You only have to read what they say about Jackie (Stewart). I don't agree with everything Jackie does. I think you owe the public, really, genuinely owe them. That doesn't mean that you have to get yourself killed to prove it. Look at "Seppi" (Siffert). Some drivers you see out on the track and there's a sort of question mark about them. You know they are going to be lucky to survive. Not Jo! He always seemed to be on top of it, like Jimmy I suppose. Who would have thought that Jimmy would get it in a Formula 2 race? Piers? (Courage)—Yes! He was always so nervous and obviously forced himself to be competitive. Jochen? (Rindt)—Okay. He drove so hard and put his car through so much there was always a chance that one day he wouldn't be able to put it all back together again.

Jochen Rindt in trouble in the Spanish Grand Prix, 1969, a year before his fatal crash at Monza.

Worst of all was von Trips. He just seemed to go from accident to accident. How many did he have at Monza before it finally killed him? Four?—Five? I don't know. It's all the same, I suppose, once you're dead. I suppose it's only in retrospect that you see all this crap about aura. Like Pedro—I think I thought it before he died. I never said anything! You can't! But it seems that I always thought that Pedro felt bad about his brother Ricardo (Rodriguez) being killed and it seemed to haunt him. I wasn't a bit surprised when I heard he was dead—inevitable!' Graham paused and looked hard at me as if expecting me to make some comment. I wasn't that foolish. Graham in full flood wasn't likely to take kindly to an outside opinion. I avoided the issue by checking the tape-recorder.

'You know,' he continued, 'since Jo died I've had more people ask me about retiring than at any time before. Even after the accident at Watkins Glen most people avoided the subject. Now everybody seems to be trying to tell me something. Why? Don't they think I know as much about what's going on as anybody? Bette makes sure I see all the bits and pieces in the paper. Christ! It's all so bloody stupid. Nothing could have saved Jo. So why is it that everybody is arguing about the marshalling and the fire-fighting equipment? Siffert's death was a motor-racing death. If you're a driver and not too stupid you have to accept that machines can fall to pieces or you can make some silly mistake and then, if everything is stacked the wrong way, cop it. What gets right up my nose is that it all becomes an intellectual exercise for people who drive nothing more dangerous than a typewriter. They sit there and say: "Right, we know what happened but—what if...", and then they spend weeks talking about all the things which didn't happen. Instead what they should say—if they really have an interest in the sport and not just in filling their columns with a load of shit—they should say: "Siffert dead". Then they should look at all the peripherals. Like why was there no phone line with Race HQ? Whose arse needs kicking because the fire extinguishers didn't work? Why is it chicken to have Armco barriers and catch fencing? Why do the organisers, who coin the money, fight the idea of having fully trained, international marshals instead of half-trained amateurs? For years the idea has been running around that maybe it's not a good idea to have a vast multi-million pound industry resting on the shoulders of unpaid enthusiasts who are as much interested in getting a front seat at the race as anything else. And who can blame them?! They know the organiser is getting a lot of cash. The Press tell them all the time about the millionaire racing drivers. Everywhere the marshal looks he sees everyone having a great time while he is expected to rush into danger for a bottle of Coke, a pork pie and his bus fare home. Motor racing should be about life, not death! If it was about death the turnover in drivers would be weekly. You don't have to do a lot at 160 miles an hour to fulfil a deathwish. What you are out there proving is that in spite of the odds, in spite of the God-awful administration, in spite of weather, faulty components and rushes of blood to the brain, you can survive.'

Graham was quiet for a while and I thought he had got it all off his chest. But he hadn't.

Scrambling was never like this! Graham negotiates a David Wynne statue temporarily parked on the lawn at Lyndhurst.

'Course the money helps. Especially once you get in amongst it. It also hinders. You begin to enjoy things you never knew existed. You want to secure that. You want to stay in there and get what you can so that sometime in the future you can retire knowing that you have done all the frantic things you wanted to do and now you can sit back and enjoy. At the moment it seems hard to believe that situation will ever come about but it still stays there in my mind. Unfortunately it's confused. I find myself thinking of all the things I'm going to do, especially family things, taking the kids around, showing them all the things I've seen. Trouble is I see them the same age as they are now. And I see myself still motor racing. It's a lack of imagination I suppose. Just can't imagine a weekend without a starting grid. Sometimes that worries me. I get a sort of tunnel vision. Literally! The future's like a gleaming tunnel, always bending to the right for some reason.

I know that around the bend there are all sorts of things happening and I can dip
into whatever's going. But while I'm in the tunnel it's just me, the car and the
noise.' He gave a cynical laugh and pushed himself to his feet.

'I suppose I think it's all bloody Monaco and I don't want to see what's around
the bend.'

Our egress was a lot more genteel than our arrival. Graham seemed to have
exorcised his demons and was back in the prize winners' circle again.

There was one other time Graham became preoccupied with death. It was
when he was waging his long running battle to have the tricycle invalid car
consigned to the museum of interesting misconceptions. He had been stamping
his foot on podiums up and down the country and had bent the ear of personages
large and small, royal and common, including that interesting hinterland of
politicians as personified at that time by Edward Heath.

Graham's rhetoric, directed at those only metaphorically in the driving seat of
the lethal 'trike' programme, was delivered on behalf of the paraplegics and other
handicapped people who gratefully accepted the means of transport without
appreciating its fragility. In the course of thudding home his message he visited a

Right *Graham doing his duty at the 1970 Sports Car Show.*

lot of centres set up to cater for the handicapped. It invariably depressed him. His time in the wheelchair, after his accident, as short as it had been, had given him a genuine sympathy for those who knew that they were there for life. He tried to alleviate the problem by working up an interest amongst the boys from the Springfield Boys' Club in Clapton, East London, of which Graham was president for many years and to which he had devoted a lot of time since the early '60s. Early in '73 he took some of the boys to meet a group of paraplegics for a get-together in a gymnasium. There was table tennis, quoits, darts, bar skittles and that sort of thing. At first the party went fairly well but gradually the fit teenagers got bored with the restrictions put on them by their hosts' limited mobility and began some noisy horse play amongst themselves. Graham gallantly tried to keep the evening going but he now had two distinct groups on his hands and much as he rushed around trying to work up mutual enthusiasm it was obvious he was on a loser.

Later in the evening he went on to the opening of a pub in north London some-where. There were a lot of people from motor racing there. As usual Graham was greeted enthusiastically and he tried to enter into the spirit of the occasion, demonstrating his trick with a cigarette, which was a bit peculiar for a non-smoker, and listening patiently to long garrulous stories which he had heard before. As the pressure on his services as the life and soul of the party decreased, he found a corner and propped himself up there. The lack of co-operation between the boys and the paraplegics was bothering him. It seemed to bring home to him the full impact of the cripple's destiny in being bound to his chair. He said that it was something he couldn't have stood. He hadn't the strength of mind to overcome the despair of knowing that he would never again be able to function in anything near a normal fashion. When he had recovered from his crash, and the doctors were making gloomy forecasts about the distinct possibility that he might not walk again, blind panic had taken over, he claimed. It was this that had fired him up to fight against the pain. He was lucky! Fairly early on he had realised that he could at least move. Then it was relatively easy to fight the pain and battle on. That didn't apply to the people who knew they would never have any movement and didn't even have pain to fight against to give them direction.

On his tours he met plenty of ex-sportsmen and others confined to wheelchairs by accidents. It made him frantic that this could happen to him. Death he reckoned he could cope with. Anyway it wasn't in his province to be able to do anything about it, and it really didn't matter how you died. The thought of being trapped in a blazing car might give you the horrors, but if the other end of the experience was death there was no problem. It was only when you were able to look back and relive the agony that it became unbearable. What anyone totally handicapped had to live with was not only the memories of life before the accident but the accident as well. It was like dying over and over again. A few years previously he had visited a friend who had broken his neck. He was completely paralysed. He had asked Graham to kill him. He couldn't bring himself even to consider it, although he knew that he would be doing his friend an act of kindness. Worst of all was the fact that he could not kill himself. Graham thought that he should have been able to supply him with the instruments to take his own life. Instead all he could do was sit there and mouth homilies about never giving up hope and assuring him that it would be all right later. He never went to see him again although he occasionally spoke to him on the telephone. Graham just couldn't bear the agony of being unable either to do something or to give him the relief he wanted.

Disability was the spectre which haunted Graham Hill and his continued flirtation with it was his own way of chasing away the bogey-man.

Chapter 9

Nothing on the clock

With Rolf Stommelen flat on his back and likely to stay there for quite a while, Graham was in a fix. He may even have regretted the cavalier way he had jettisoned Guy Edwards, who was going ahead with his court case to secure redress. As ever, Hill was keeping tight-lipped about his future plans as a racing driver. Once again, in 1975, there was trouble with the Monaco entry. Fears for the continuance of road racing were revived with a vengeance after the tragedy in Montjuich Parque. Aware that a panic reaction could have adverse effects on motor racing's showcase, the organisers, this time with the blessing of the GPDA, agreed to cut the entry from 22 to 18. It meant there would be a lot of idle machinery on Sunday but it would prove the point that the interested parties were firm in their resolve to make motor racing safer.

Realistically, Graham only entered one car for Monaco, a GH2 with himself in the hot seat. It would have been unthinkable to have anyone but the maestro behind the wheel for the race that he had made his own. With his record it seemed that he was bound to do well, probably better than at any other circuit in the world. Monaco is not a fast track, it's too small and windy to get up a good head of steam, but it needs finesse. Hill could supply this, only he didn't get the chance. The faster of the two cars he took to the race swallowed a valve in practice and he had to switch to the older, less athletic car. In this he didn't stand a dog's chance, not with the bustling newcomers haunched down and ready to spring to finish off the last of the old brigade. Nikki Lauda was setting Ferrari up for a big, overdue comeback. Britain's Tom Pryce, one of the best extractions from the over-subscribed club calendar, was showing form which had rival team managers nervously fingering their lap charts and, of course, there was no disputing the talent of ex-World Champion Emerson Fittipaldi, world champion pretender Ronnie Peterson, maniac marauder Clay Regazzoni, Scheckter, Pace, Reutemann, Britain's pop star James Hunt and the glittering galaxy of drivers surrounding them, all of them seemingly within nail-biting distance of the Grand Pot.

To the distress of Prince Rainier and Princess Grace, who saw Graham as one of their established tourist traps, and to the disappointment of his thousands of fans, Hill was left to watch the race through the wire mesh of the safety fencing. He put on a good face and even made a brief appearance at his old stomping ground, the Tip-Top Bar, but it was easy to see how bitterly disappointed he was.

Above *'Mr Monaco' in pensive mood.*   **Above right** *Triumph at Monaco in 1968.*
Below *Even Graham passed up this challenge!*

Monaco was Graham's high. His annual moment of deification. To not win was an affront but to not qualify . . . The Monégasques and the visitor-strewn balconies didn't seem to care. Graham Hill was Graham Hill, whether he was driving or not didn't matter.

At the peak of his career he had been given an ovation, as he walked to the pits, such as few people get without leading the parade up the main drag with a conquering army for escort. On race day Graham would time his walk from the Hotel de Paris to the pits with calculated nonchalance, not so early as to miss the crowds on the balconies which, being less controllable than the bums on the public seats, only took up position when things started to happen, and not so late that he had to hurry. At the appropriate moment, Graham, Bette and anybody who happened to be with him would slip out of the barricaded back door of the hotel, and be ushered through the high, corrugated iron security barrier and on to the Armco-lined road leading down to the pits. Graham was at his best. Gleaming white in his flame-proof overalls, unmistakable battle helmet swinging by the strap, he strode down the hill like a Grade A knight about to give an exhibition of jousting to the local, sub-standard nobility, and the crowd loved it. He had many imitators but the fans knew margarine from butter and were not fooled. Even when Jackie Stewart tried to upstage him by doing the walk, accompanied not only by the delectable Helen but also by a well-padded Elizabeth Taylor, the applause was in sympathy for a good try. Graham's walk, for most of the regulars, was the official benediction on the race. They had seen 'Mr. Monaco', the champagne was on ice and the TV tuned in for the bits of the race out of range of the high soaring terraces. The spectacle could begin.

In contrast, Monaco '75 was bitter for Graham Hill, and although he still got instant adulation wherever he went, it burned into him that it was for past glories, and would soon fade. The decision to retire, postponed because of Stommelen's accident, was being forced on him and he didn't like it. The question which tortured Graham relentlessly was whether or not it was possible to make the last grandstand gesture that would let him retire while still a contender. His conflict was between his rational, experienced self and the idolised public image put over by the magazines. On one hand they were saying he was over the hill and should retire, while at the same time fanning the flames of his ambition by hinting that he might still work something out. As he often said—what else was he going to do on Sunday afternoon?

This was a desperate time for Graham. He was over-extended and buffeted by decisions that were being forced on him and giving him no time to collect himself and plot a way ahead. He was also shackled by his own self-image. Although he frequently gave lip service to the idea of going to the experts for advice, he only accepted advice which concurred with, or was compatible with, his own decisions. It made for a lot of mistakes and increased the pressure. One thing he knew for certain. Money wasn't getting any easier! The harder he worked the more he seemed to stand still. His irrascible nature became more cruel and he began to create enemies where he had had only friends and fans before. Gone were the days when Graham would sit around the paddock for hours after a race,

Trophy room or office? It was all the same to Graham. It was there, amongst the colourful memorabilia and awards that Graham did his wheeling and dealing.

signing autographs and chatting to the hundreds of devotees who would sidle up and just stare at the man who had, against the odds, eclipsed Fangio, Clark and Moss in the public eye. Now he would storm around his equipe, making bitter, cutting comments for little or no reason, and then stalk off to the Aztec and leave the circuit.

The biggest monkey on his back was his retirement. He had known he had to make a decision for a long time. Bitterly he remembered the times he could have done it with panache. Now it looked as if his glorious career, encompassing 176 Grands Prix, two world championships, the Indianaplis 500 and the famous Le Mans, plus countless Formula 2, sports car and saloon car races and practically every other type of motorised sport, including records for speed over measured distances, was going to end, not with a bang but a whimper. For a while he entertained the thought that the Belgian Grand Prix might provide the setting for his finale. It was the sort of circuit he had done well on in the past. A circuit where skill and experience mattered. Again he studied the facts. Skill and experience he had—in trumps! Unfortunately it was crammed into an envelope forty-six years old.

While Graham had mooned around Monaco in gloomy rejection he had noted the Formula 3 performance of a young man from Bexley in Kent, twenty-three-year-old Tony Brise. He had graduated to potential stardom along the road

Above left *A relaxed Graham Hill introduces his new driver, Tony Brise, to the public. May 1975.*
Above right *Tony and Janet Brise.*

pioneered by such stalwarts as Fittipaldi and Peterson. A child phenomenon at karting at the age of ten, he later came, via Formula 3 and Atlantic, to a one-off appearance in the ill-fated Barcelona race. Tyrrell, Chapman and Surtees had all cast a favourable eye over the young Kentish man but it was Hill, anxious to be able to state something unequivocal to his sponsors, who slapped a contract down and got a signature. Hill tried to kid himself that he would be in the second car but when he arrived at the Belgian circuit and reflected on what had to be done he sensibly decided to practise his role of team-manager some more. He still wasn't making any announcements about retiring and for once the Press showed some respect for the mental agony he was going through. Everybody knew in their heart of hearts that 'Jake' was prevaricating.

Brise gave Hill a shot in the arm. He listened attentively to what Hill had to say and then went out on the track and laid down a performance consistent with the possibilities of the car. Graham responded instantly to the new relationship. He was too cautious to go over the top too soon but the rapport he had with his new driver, and the faith he had in his own ability, gave him a breathing space, the quiet he needed for the decision that had haunted him since 1969. With regret he withdrew from the Belgian Grand Prix and directed his attention to getting his young protégé off to a good start. Brise's tenth place qualification for the grid was satisfying and his performance at the start of the race before being sidelined was reassuring. In the couple of weeks leading up to the Dutch Grand Prix Graham began to get the glint back in his eye. In spite of the fact that once again he was consigned to the coach's bench he felt there was a forward movement, a justification for the statements he had been making about encouraging young drivers and combining his circuit wizardry with their youth and sharp reflexes to build a race winner. On the 'Noah's Ark' grid Tony Brise qualified for the fourth row beside none other than double World Champion Emerson Fittipaldi himself. In the second Embassy/Hill was future World Champion Alan Jones, who was five rows back.

The day was to be a great fillip for British pretensions to world motor racing domination. James Hunt won in a Hesketh-Ford and nearly gave the noble Lord Alexander a heart attack with delight. Tony Brise gave notice of his intention to stir up the establishment by finishing just outside the points in seventh place behind Welshman Tom Pryce in the uncompetitive UOP Shadow. Aussie Alan Jones proved the Embassy/Hill's reliability by keeping his car going to claim thirteenth place. It was good enough to let Graham make his decision with grace. His retirement was still supposed to be a deep, dire secret but people were beginning to wonder if he had retired and nobody had noticed, especially when the entries for the French Grand Prix at the sun-baked hotplate of Paul Ricard were posted. Brise had taken Stommelen's entry and Alan Jones was once more deputising for Graham.

Bette shows relief when Graham officially bows out of racing before the British Grand Prix at Silverstone. Graham's wink seems to suggest something more.

Again Brise did exceptionally well to qualify on the fifth row of the grid on an unfamiliar circuit, especially beside the Argentinian tyro Carlos Reutemann with Jones four rows behind. Graham nervously paced the pits while his man stroked his GH2 home to another incident-free seventh place. Jones proved that the Embassy car was stuck together properly by finishing—albeit at the back of the field. That really was the topper! Now Graham could go ahead and plan for Silverstone.

To nobody's surprise but his own, Graham's farewell tour of the Silverstone circuit was an emotional moment in a sport that disdains emotion of any sort and can shrug off the death of one of its participants without an apparent second thought. But to the men and boys—and ladies—in the bleachers it was like losing a close relative. The majority of those present had grown up thinking that the name 'Graham Hill' was a permanent fixture in the programme. His carefully manicured moustache, slicked back hair and white slashed helmet were as recognisable to the man in the street as to *aficionados*. As he circled the track at Silverstone in his own Embassy GH2 for the last time it was as if he was receiving an honorary Oscar. The one race that he would dearly have loved to win was his native British Grand Prix. There had been moments when he had almost managed it but it had always slipped away from him. To the cheering fans in the stands that didn't matter. They were relieved that he had decided to call it a day. He had faced death so often on their behalf that they were happy to have the chance of giving him the thumbs up. Even if he hadn't won a Grand Prix at Silverstone, at least he had won a non-championship race there, and that only a

President of the British Racing Drivers Club, HRH the Duke of Edinburgh, gets a few suggestions from one of its most illustrious members at Silverstone 1975.

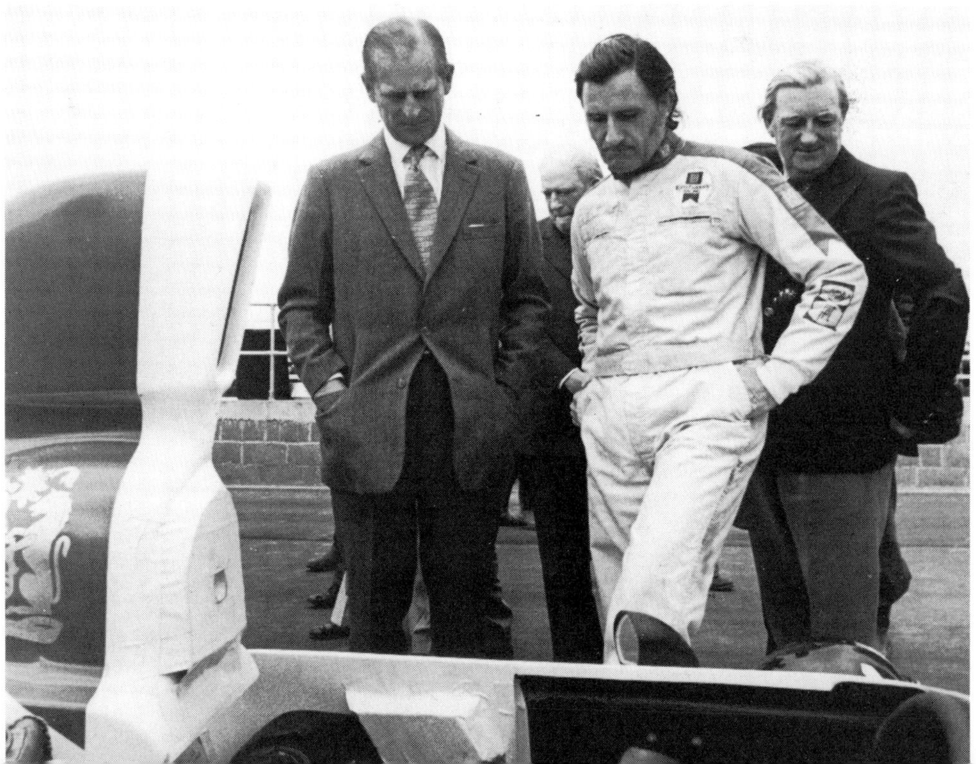

couple of years before. In the pits the drivers, team managers, mechanics, marshals and all those who had been involved with Graham over the years crowded to the barriers and clapped and cheered him on his way. As he went round he must have thought back over the disappointments of his British Grands Prix efforts: the early promises of success, fourth in '62, third in '63, second in '64 and '65, third again in '66, the race well in hand in '67 when his suspension collapsed, another suspension collapse robbing him of the lead in '68, fuel the villain in '69 and the humiliating start-line shunt when Jack Oliver ran up his exhaust pipe on the grid in '71. But that was all behind him now! His future lay in producing a team that was a world-beater. The mix of the Hills and Brises was a happy one. Janet got on well with Bette and Tony had the attitude and mental outlook that put him in harmony with Graham. It was the sort of happy situation that Graham needed to sort out all the swirling flotsam of his life. He was now able to set about bringing some order to the chaos of his ever full diary.

A few weeks after the British Grand Prix, I went over to Porters Park and played a round of golf with him. He was a changed person. The old nonchalance was back, the dry humour and the gamesmanship that had always made golf a small war. I kept off the area of his retirement. In the past it had been a touchy subject. We spoke about flying and Graham's part as a helicopter pilot in the new Alistair MacLean film *Caravan to Vaccares*, and he said that it had refired his ambition to get a rotary licence to add to his fixed wing. The future all seemed clear to him now. There was none of the sour anger at getting old and losing his remarkable powers of concentration. He said that when he had played golf with Jack Nicklaus a short while before he had remarked how much he admired the top golfers, and how all the other sportsmen took up golf because it satisfied their

Graham discovers that a lot of water has flowed under the bridge since he stroked a crew, 1975.

competitive nature, while at the same time, through the handicap system, making it possible to play on equal terms, while they learned with more capable players. Nicklaus agreed with Graham but argued that it wasn't the supreme test of character that a lot of people claimed it to be. It lacked one vital element—danger! The biggest danger in golf, Nicklaus claimed, was that he might sprain his ankle on a divot. Motor racing, on the other hand, demanded total concentration, strength, stamina, intelligence and a huge helping of courage, because every time a driver eased out onto a track he knew he was flirting with death—the added dimension that put it beyond any other type of sport, with the possible exception of bullfighting and gladiatorial combat.

Graham's reaction to leaving it all behind seemed to be mixed. On the surface he appeared relaxed and confident. But the readiness with which he discussed his retirement spoke volumes. Driving back to Lyndhurst he was in an expansive mood. Offers were flowing in from all quarters. At last he felt sure he had got the hang of it all. He would make selected charity appearances for free but charge a fee for everything else. He was particularly hopeful about his connection with CBS in the States. He had had an on/off relationship with them for some time but now he was less under pressure on the driving front, they were talking about more varied fields for him to explore as a personality rather than as a racing helmet. The subject of the fruitful oil fields of the Middle East had even been broached. Discussions were in progress about a circuit and a wealthy sheik was interested in backing a new type of international magazine. Everything in the Hill garden seemed to be lovely!

It was the last time I saw Graham. Shortly afterwards, I left for Argentina to work on a film. The local interest being what it was, I kept abreast of what was

As a racing driver Paul Newman makes a fine actor, as he demonstrates to Graham here.

Above left *Samantha gets the rudiments of bike control from the expert.*
Above right *Breaking in a new flat 'at, Graham Hill takes over the role of commentator.*

going on through the well-informed magazines. The Embassy team seemed to be getting it together. For a new marque, the car was going as well as could be expected. There was a tremor towards the end of the season when there seemed to be some doubt as to whether or not WD & HO Wills were going to pick up the tab for the coming year but then it was announced that they would, though for only one car. Graham made a statement claiming diplomatically that this was a 'good thing' as it would allow the team to concentrate on the singleton entry for Tony Brise. It all seemed perfectly calm and straightforward. Then came the tragic news.

I had just spent an infuriating, futile week in Uruguay searching for film locations which I was assured existed but somehow had failed to materialise. On the way back, the car windscreen had shattered and I had to drive about 150 miles in furnace-like heat and flaying dust only to spend about four hours in the customs sheds in Buenos Aires because of some minor irregularity in the car's papers which hadn't been spotted in Colonia. By the time I got to the office in Avenida 25 de Mayo I was exhausted. As I went in the receptionist said she was sorry to hear about Graham. She was amazed that I didn't know as it was the biggest news in Argentina at that time. Fervent Hill fans to a man, they had taken the tragedy as if he were one of their own. I rang the local TV station where I worked on and off and asked them for details. They filled me in on what they knew and suggested I went on the air and gave an appreciation of Hill, the man and the driver.

I was exhausted and shattered. I just wanted to get away somewhere and think. Walking along under the arches beside the Avenida del Libertador running by the Rio de la Plata my thoughts were pretty morbid. It seemed unbelievable after the life that Graham had lived, permanently at risk, that death should claim him a few paltry months after retirement. Details at the time were sketchy. It seemed that he had broken rule one and flown into a non-controlled airfield when even the most foolhardy crows were clutching tight to the lower branches of the smaller trees. Why had he taken that uncharacteristic chance and paid the penalty with his life and those of his five companions? Was he so short of thrills in his new job of team manager that he took deliberate, stupid chances to get the charge he was missing in his day to day life? It seems unlikely.

Flyers all have a deeply held reluctance to put themselves in an untenable situation. From the first time they turn over a propeller they get an ingrained respect for the pull of gravity and nothing short of a brainstorm will allow them to treat it lightly. What does happen is a razor edge decision falls the wrong way. A weather report is read with the bias on the wrong side. Maybe the 4 octas of cloud are stacked adversely, or the precipitation factor is marginally adrift precisely where you want it to be right on. Whatever the reason, Graham ignored suggestions to abandon the last stage of his journey back to Elstree. What happened then can only be reconstructed from the accident report prepared by the Civil Aviation Authorities. With precious little to go on beyond a few words of conversation with ground-based radio operators and controllers, plus the readings shown on the flight instruments at impact, the CAA conclusion is necessarily vague.

On November 29 1975 Graham was putting the new Embassy/Hill through its paces at the Le Castellet circuit of Paul Ricard. The previous day he had flown down in his Aztec, had an early night and spent the day trying to sort out whatever problems they were having, in an attempt to put Tony Brise on the grid of the 1976 Grands Prix with a sporting chance. The day had been without traumas. There was still a lot to do on the car but now they had found a fair degree of reliability, it was safe to assume that agility would follow. Graham was reasonably happy with the result, so, as darkness settled over the area, he called it a day and offered the five vacant seats on his plane to Tony Brise and the other members of his team. Suitcases, spare parts and racing paraphernalia made the plane a little overweight but there was adequate runway length and the excess would be burned off as the fuel was used in flight, so the landing weight would be well inside that recommended in the book.

At Marseilles Graham topped up the fuel and set out for Elstree, estimating his arrival time there at 22:00 hrs—a four hour journey. The flight navigation was faultless and, helped by obliging winds, he arrived over Dover about 25 minutes early. From available information, he was aware that the conditions at Elstree were marginally against him and was given further information on his flight from

45 Yankee; *the Piper Aztec bought with the money from the 1965 Indy win, and the Formula 1 BRM.*

Dover to the Lambourne VOR, (a radio-navigation aid just outside Abridge in Essex) that the weather was getting rapidly worse around the London area. Above 1500 ft the sky was clear but below it the forward visibility was less than 2500 m which is not far when you are travelling at 200 mph. Just before reaching Lambourne, while flying at approximately 8000 ft, he contacted London Air Traffic Control Centre and was given permission to descend to 4000 ft.

Asked what he intended to do, in view of the deteriorating conditions at Elstree, Graham said he would have a look at Elstree and if he didn't like what he saw would divert to Luton where conditions were marginally better, and where he could at least have more direct help in getting onto the deck. At Elstree, the nearest aid was about 10 miles south-west at Heathrow and could only help at a distance. So far everything was running to schedule. The only problem looming was getting down through a fog 1500 ft thick to land on a tiny strip of tarmac.

The flight presented no problems. He had made it many times before. There were plenty of alternatives he could pick where there were more facilities. When Graham first contacted the London Air Traffic Control he was told that all was not well at his terminal airport. The visibility above the fog was down to 2000 m with a cloudbase of 330 ft above ground level, about twice the height of Nelson's Column. Graham was determined to have a look at the situation and then decide whether he should divert to Luton or some other airport with navigational aids and long accommodating runways. The flight from Dover to Lambourne was uneventful, although he was off the air for ten minutes, probably listening to the continuously broadcast Volmet weather report. When he re-established contact he was given permission to descend from his in-passage flight level of 80 (approximately 8000 ft) to 4000 ft. He was also told that visibility was now down to 800 m.

At Lambourne he turned west towards Elstree and was given clearance to descend to 1500 ft. Lambourne is approximately 19 miles from Elstree with nothing apparently viciously lethal in between. A few minutes later Graham reported that he was level at 1500 ft. He had now changed frequency to London Approach at Heathrow, who were giving him assistance in lining up on Elstree 12 miles or so to the north. There are errors in most navigational equipment. For general navigation they aren't much of a bother but working at a distance, with the natural lag of verbal communication, the information can only be imprecise. There were still seemingly no problems. At 1500 ft the Aztec would have been in cloud but the lights below would have been visible.

At 4 miles to touchdown the London Approach operator informed him that he was on his own. He could not give more assistance within the known inaccuracy tolerance of the equipment and the marginal errors of height and heading that the pilot could be expected to make. Evidently Graham then switched to the Elstree radio frequency. This is a purely advisory service. It cannot give flight instruction or accurate environment information beyond barometer readings and wind direction and strength. The rest is down to the pilot's interpretation of what the radio operator tells him. Graham told the tower that he was on finals. He was told that the barometric setting on his altimetre, which would give him his height above the runway, was 990 mb and that he was clear to land. All that was heard after that was a 'Four/Five', the last two digits of his callsign without the final 'Y' for 'Yankee'. It is believed that this was the precise moment that he struck the trees and crashed in a ball of flame into Arkley Golf Course.

Epilogue

What caused Graham, an experienced and careful pilot with 1600 hours to his credit, to plunge into trees 120 ft above runway level and 3 miles short of the runway? No one will ever know for certain. The Civil Aviation Authority made a thorough and expert evaluation of all the facts and admitted themselves baffled. In the final analysis it seemed to be pilot error. Another case of a pilot trying to do more than was within his capabilities. Disorientated in the fog he had mistaken the golf course for the airfield. It seemed a reasonable assumption.

As an exercise in futility I recently decided to set up the instruments on another aircraft and, in clear daylight, flew Graham's last route to see if it was possible to discover what ill chance had written a final ending to one of the great post-war heroes of sport. Bette Hill asked if she could come along to see what happened.

What we were going to do wasn't going to be remotely like what Graham had experienced. For one thing he was flying a twin-engined Aztec and we were in a single-engined Arrow, and there was no way I was going to risk my neck swanning around after dark in a pea-souper. Other things were different. Graham had a QFE on his altimetre of 990 mb. The day we went, the setting was 1001 mb, and it was broad daylight. I picked up the Lambourne VOR and turned west. The radial from the beacon to Elstree is approximately 277 degrees. In Graham's plane the navigational equipment had been all but destroyed by fire but the investigators had managed to discover that his Receiver No 1 was reading 312 degrees and No 2 had 266 degrees. Assuming that 312 was the radial to Lambourne, the probability is that the 266 setting was meant to be the radial from Lambourne to Elstree. So if he was navigating on the No 2 receiver and had fed in the wrong information where would that put us?

I dialled up 266 degrees and, maintaining a prudent 1500 ft, turned west. The error to Elstree (277 degrees) would be about 011 degrees. That line of reasoning got us nowhere. We finished up heading into the London CTR and three or four miles away from the crash site. It was obvious that taking the 266 degrees radial out of Lambourne was not the answer. The investigators found that the equipment was so burned that they hadn't been able to identify what frequency the equipment had been set at. Where did you get to if you back-tracked 266? The answer is the VOR at Clacton. Clacton VOR's frequency is 115.7. Lambourne's is 115.6! Could Graham have been using the Clacton beacon in his attempt to navigate to Elstree?

At first it seems unlikely. Clacton is over 50 miles from Elstree while Lambourne is only 18. But Lambourne VOR is the Doppler type warned against by the CAA. In some conditions the Lambourne VOR can give some very inaccurate readings. I have personally experienced this on a couple of occasions. So, could it be possible that Graham wasn't happy with the response he was getting from Lambourne and had switched to Clacton believing he would get a better reading, even at the longer range, than he was getting from Lambourne? And if he had, where would that put us in respect to Arkley Golf Course? Believe it or not—less than 1 mile north of Arkley! Now take into account the fact that Class 1 radio equipment is reckoned to have an accuracy of plus or minus 5 degrees and you can say that the route would fly straight across the crash site. This proved to be the case when we tried it out. We went back to the 312 degrees on the No 1 set. Back-tracking, that put us on to the Detling VOR. This is located north-west of Dover, 10 miles south of the route from Dover to Lambourne. Conceivably Graham could have dialled up a radial from Detling to Elstree (312°) to give him two radials; Detling and either Lambourne or Clacton; to shepherd him into the Elstree area. It seems a bit unnecessary and it's difficult to see why he should do it when he could more easily get a cross reference from handier beacons, but you do a lot of funny things to while away the tedium of a long flight. On balance the probability must be that he just hadn't bothered to

Just a few of the trophies that come the way of a World Champion.

change the setting of his leg from Dover to Lambourne. There was no reason to do so.

What happened at Arkley when he hit the trees at 458 ft when he should have been about 1,000 ft higher? Again we will never be able to sort that out. Probably it had something to do with an incorrect setting on the altimeter. Elstree threshold is 334 ft above sea level, 1 mb = approximately 27 ft, so the barometric pressure at Elstree is roughly 12 mb less than at sea level.

In aviation sea level is quoted as QNH. It is always higher than, or occasionally equal to, the QFE which is the pressure at airfield level. There is a further altimeter setting. This is only used when flying airways, usually 6000 ft or above. It's known as QNE and is arbitrarily set internationally at a constant 1013 mb. Could Graham, somehow, have made a mistake when switching from one setting to another? Is it possible that after flying on QNE at flight level 80 he forgot to change to the QNH of 1002, but believed himself to be flying on that setting? In that case he would be roughly 300 ft lower than he thought. When he hit the trees he had already called 'Finals!' and was descending at a steady rate of around 300 ft per minute. This would mean that he would descend from a height of just over 600 ft in 2 minutes. At 95 mph he would travel about 3 miles. The crash site is exactly 3 miles from Elstree.

A wild assumption would be that he was flying on QNE believing it to be QNH. Because of this he was 330 ft or more lower than he believed. In the confusion of the heavy workload brought on by deteriorating conditions and with probably a touch of spatial disorientation brought on by trying to fly on the instruments while at the same time make sense of the lights dimly seen through the mist, he mistook the QNH passed to him by London Control to be the QFE; the setting for landing at Elstree. At about 4 miles from Elstree he started his descent and informed Elstree that he was on finals. Elstree told him he was free to land and added a precautionary 'check three greens' which means that the wheels were down and locked. This is a usual reminder from the operator. Graham started to reply and went off the air. It is supposed that this was the moment of first impact.

The time, the height and the distance from Elstree threshold are all consistent with the altimeters having been on the wrong setting. There is no inconsistency in the Aztec's approach to Elstree. Whether Graham was using the Clacton VOR or was relying solely on London Approach to lead him home doesn't matter. The altitude was the critical factor. Having flown the route and being familiar with the area from flying in and out of Elstree on a regular basis, it seems the only answer.

Bette seemed to benefit from the flight even if our conclusions weren't conclusive and came not one iota closer to helping Graham avoid the fatal accident. It seemed to exorcise some of the ghosts which had hung over her since that fateful night when she had heard the terrible news. Just flying over the route and seeing it from the air on a bright autumn day helped to alleviate some of the sorrow of the past years.

Afterword by Damon Hill

There is a photograph in our house, which is kept in that certain place where we can all fully appreciate good humour; the WC. It shows my father giving a specific hand signal (which used to be known as the 'Harvey Smith') to an American commentator at Watkins Glen, when the poor misguided chap had the lack of insight to suggest that it might be about time that Graham Hill, at 44 years of age and after 156 Grands Prix, should objectively consider retirement. This might sound at first as though it was a little less than respectful, and certainly not diplomatic on my father's part. However, if you could see the picture, I will defy anybody to show me a face in it that is not already straining under the effects of a wide grin, if not broken wide open by laughter.

I think that if I had to pick one aspect which I remember best of my father, then it would be his humour. It was this which would transcend all barriers, social, emotional and circumstantial. I believe it was this which enabled him to deal with nearly all situations; because he could laugh at himself. In fact, what made him so lovable was that often he would deliberately send himself up.

I can remember once at a Pro/Am golf tournament, he was coming to the last hole and the caddie went to hand him his putter. He told him not to give it to him yet but to wait until it was his putt, and to keep it in the bag until then. There was, of course, a fairly large gathering of spectators encircling the green, waiting quietly and patiently, appreciating each players' attempts at putting small white balls in small white holes. The atmosphere was tense, and one could almost hear people wishing that their favourite hero would, just this once, play a clean stroke so they could go home without too many shattered illusions. Finally, it was Daddy's turn to play. He slowly and deliberately drew his putter from the golf bag, strode (as best he could) out to his ball, and addressed it, ready to put it away in the hole. However, because of his inquisitive and innovative nature, he had a special custom-made putter which was barely 2 ft long. This, he protested, was guaranteed to make him putt better, because he was closer to the ball; but it also had something to do with his broken legs. Anyhow, it produced, as one would expect, rampant hilarity amongst the crowd. And of course, he took a little longer over the putt than was necessary, just to ham it up a while longer. I can't remember if he holed it or not.

Golf was something which I liked to play with him, possibly because I could almost be guaranteed a couple of hours with him, on our own, without the phone

going and me having to listen to one end of a conversation (which I enjoyed doing anyway). Another, more social way of achieving the same end, was to go shooting, which he enjoyed tremendously, and I was always more than willing to come along. It really was as if he was more at home with a shotgun than behind the wheel. When we were shooting, racing was a thousand miles away. To me it seemed that racing was work, what Daddy did for a living, which is true to a degree. I don't think he was as happy with racing as he had been in the early days. But I know how much he loved to race a car.

When he retired in 1975, at his official Press announcement at Silverstone before the British Grand Prix, he asked me what I thought of his decision. At first I said I didn't really know yet. 'Don't you think it's a little sad?' he asked, almost emotionally. 'I suppose so', I mumbled. He probably then worried about having an idiot for a son, but the truth was that I was quite pleased really. I loved him and didn't want to lose him. Now we wouldn't have to worry about him not coming home every other week. I didn't really appreciate how much he loved racing then. Otherwise, I would have really understood how sad he must have been, after so long, to give up a part of himself, which so many years before had driven him to give up nearly everything just to race a car. Typical.

Damon Hill shared a love of motor bikes with his father and now races them on the track.

Appendix

Major race results 1958-74

1958

Monaco (Formula 1 and Grand Prix debut)	Did not finish

1960

Dutch Grand Prix	3rd

1961

French Grand Prix	6th
US Grand Prix	5th

1962

Dutch Grand Prix	1st
Monaco Grand Prix	6th
Belgian Grand Prix	2nd
French Grand Prix	9th
British Grand Prix	4th
German Grand Prix	1st
Italian Grand Prix	1st
US Grand Prix	2nd
South African Grand Prix	1st

WORLD CHAMPION

1963

Monaco Grand Prix	1st
Belgian Grand Prix	Did not finish
Dutch Grand Prix	Did not finish
French Grand Prix	3rd
British Grand Prix	3rd
German Grand Prix	Did not finish
Italian Grand Prix	16th
US Grand Prix	1st
Mexican Grand Prix	4th

3rd in World Championship

1964

Monaco Grand Prix	1st
Dutch Grand Prix	4th
Belgian Grand Prix	5th
French Grand Prix	2nd
British Grand Prix	2nd
German Grand Prix	2nd
Austrian Grand Prix	Did not finish
Italian Grand Prix	Did not finish
US Grand Prix	1st
Mexican Grand Prix	11th

2nd in World Championship

1965

Dutch Grand Prix	3rd
Monaco Grand Prix	1st
Belgian Grand Prix	5th
French Grand Prix	5th
British Grand Prix	2nd
Dutch Grand Prix	4th
German Grand Prix	2nd
Italian Grand Prix	2nd
US Grand Prix	1st
Mexican Grand Prix	Did not finish

2nd in World Championship

1966

Monaco Grand Prix	3rd
Belgian Grand Prix	Did not finish
French Grand Prix	Did not finish
British Grand Prix	3rd
Dutch Grand Prix	2nd

German Grand Prix   4th
Italian Grand Prix   Did not
                         finish
US Grand Prix   14th
Mexican Grand Prix   Did not
                         finish

5th in World Championship
Winner of Indianapolis 500

1967
South African Grand Prix   Did not
                            finish
Monaco Grand Prix   2nd
Dutch Grand Prix   Did not
                            finish
Belgian Grand Prix   Did not
                            finish
French Grand Prix   Did not
                            finish
British Grand Prix   Did not
                            finish
German Grand Prix   Did not
                            finish
Canadian Grand Prix   4th
Italian Grand Prix   Did not
                            finish
US Grand Prix   2nd
Mexican Grand Prix   Did not
                            finish

6th in World Championship

1968
South African Grand Prix   2nd
Spanish Grand Prix   1st
Monaco Grand Prix   1st
Belgian Grand Prix   Did not
                            finish
Dutch Grand Prix   9th
French Grand Prix   Did not
                            finish
British Grand Prix   Did not
                            finish
German Grand Prix   2nd
Italian Grand Prix   Did not
                            finish
Canadian Grand Prix   4th
US Grand Prix   2nd
Mexican Grand Prix   1st

WORLD CHAMPION

1969
South African Grand Prix   2nd
Spanish Grand Prix   Did not
                            finish
Monaco Grand Prix   1st
Dutch Grand Prix   7th
French Grand Prix   6th
British Grand Prix   7th
German Grand Prix   4th
Italian Grand Prix   9th
Canadian Grand Prix   Did not
                            finish
US Grand Prix   Did not
                            finish

7th in World Championship

1970
South African Grand Prix   6th
Spanish Grand Prix   4th
Monaco Grand Prix   5th
Belgian Grand Prix   Did not
                            finish
Dutch Grand Prix   12th
French Grand Prix   10th
British Grand Prix   6th
German Grand Prix   Did not
                            finish
Austrian Grand Prix   No entry
US Grand Prix   Did not
                            finish
Mexican Grand Prix   Did not
                            finish

12th in World Championship

1971
South African Grand Prix   9th
Spanish Grand Prix   Did not
                            finish
Monaco Grand Prix   Did not
                            finish
Dutch Grand Prix   10th
French Grand Prix   Did not
                            finish
British Grand Prix   Did not
                            finish
German Grand Prix   9th
Austrian Grand Prix   5th
Italian Grand Prix   11th

Canadian Grand Prix   Did not finish
US Grand Prix   7th
21st in World Championship

1972
Argentinian Grand Prix   Did not finish
South African Grand Prix   6th
Spanish Grand Prix   10th
Monaco Grand Prix   12th
Belgian Grand Prix   Did not finish
French Grand Prix   10th
British Grand Prix   Did not finish
German Grand Prix   6th
Austrian Grand Prix   Did not finish
Italian Grand Prix   5th
Canadian Grand Prix   8th
US Grand Prix   11th
12th in World Championship
Winner of Le Mans

1973
Argentinian Grand Prix   No entry
Brazilian Grand Prix   No entry
South African Grand Prix   No entry
Spanish Grand Prix   Did not finish
Belgian Grand Prix   9th
Monaco Grand Prix   Did not finish

Swedish Grand Prix   Did not finish
French Grand Prix   10th
British Grand Prix   Did not finish
Dutch Grand Prix   Did not finish
German Grand Prix   13th
Austrian Grand Prix   Did not finish
Italian Grand Prix   14th
Canadian Grand Prix   16th
US Grand Prix   13th
Not classified for World Championship

1974
Argentinian Grand Prix   Did not finish
Brazilian Grand Prix   11th
South African Grand Prix   12th
Spanish Grand Prix   Did not finish
Belgian Grand Prix   8th
Monaco Grand Prix   7th
Swedish Grand Prix   6th
Dutch Grand Prix   Did not finish
French Grand Prix   13th
British Grand Prix   13th
German Grand Prix   9th
Italian Grand Prix   8th
Canadian Grand Prix   14th
US Grand Prix   8th
18th in World Championship

Index

The gang's all here. Graham, Bette, Brigitte, Samantha and Damon prepare to board a flight for a holiday in Tunisia in 1971.